The Newbie's Diabetic Air Fryer Cookbook

Discover Your Essential Guide to Guilt-Free, Low-Carb Recipes for Delicious, Blood Sugar-Friendly Meals and Improved Diabetes Management

Dannette Devore

© **Copyright 2023 - All rights reserved.**

The content contained within this book may not be reproduced, duplicated or transmitted without direct written permission from the author or the publisher.

Under no circumstances will any blame or legal responsibility be held against the publisher, or author, for any damages, reparation, or monetary loss due to the information contained within this book. Either directly or indirectly.

Legal Notice:

This book is copyright protected. This book is only for personal use. You cannot amend, distribute, sell, use, quote or paraphrase any part, or the content within this book, without the consent of the author or publisher.

Disclaimer Notice:

Please note the information contained within this document is for educational and entertainment purposes only. All effort has been executed to present accurate, up to date, and reliable, complete information. No warranties of any kind are declared or implied. Readers acknowledge that the author is not engaging in the rendering of legal, financial, medical or professional advice. The content within this book has been derived from various sources. Please consult a licensed professional before attempting any techniques outlined in this book. By reading this document, the reader agrees that under no circumstances is the author responsible for any losses, direct or indirect, which are incurred as a result of the use of information contained within this document, including, but not limited to, — errors, omissions, or inaccuracies.

Table of Contents

INTRODUCTION 6
- UNDERSTANDING DIABETES 6
- THE TWO TYPES OF DIABETES 6
- HOW TO PREVENT IT? 7
- IS AIR FRYER GOOD FOR DIABETICS? 8
- RECIPES INDEX 8

CHAPTER 1: BREAKFAST RECIPES 10
- Tofu Scramble 10
- Fried Egg 10
- Spinach and Tomato Frittata 11
- Herb Frittata 11
- Grilled Cheese 12
- Grilled Sandwich With Three Types Of Cheese 12
- Tasty Chicken Patties 13
- Scallion Sandwich 13
- Santa Fe Style Pizza 14
- Egg Croquettes 15
- Breakfast Cookies 15
- Banana Muffins 16
- Morning Sausage Patties 17
- Egg Bites 17
- Asparagus Omelet 18
- Baked Eggs 19
- Pumpkin Pie French Toast 19
- Scrambled Egg 20
- Breakfast Cheese Bread Cups 20

CHAPTER 2: MEAT RECIPES 21
- Herbed Lamb Chops 21
- Spicy Lamb Sirloin Steak 21
- Garlic Rosemary Lamb Chops 22
- Steak Bites with Mushrooms 23
- Italian-Style Beef Meatballs 23
- Meatloaf 24
- Cheeseburger Pockets 25
- Hamburgers 25
- Crispy Empanadas 26
- Diabetic-Friendly Meatballs 27

- Low-Fat Steak 27
- Beef with Mushrooms 28
- Beef Korma Curry 29
- Lemon Greek Beef and Vegetables 29
- Cracker Barrel Meatloaf 30
- Steak Wrapped Asparagus 31
- Garlic Butter Steaks 31
- Mongolian Beef Air Fryer Recipe 31
- Meatloaf Slider Wraps 32
- Double Cheeseburger 33
- Beef Schnitzel 33
- Diabetic-Friendly Meatloaf 34
- Steak with Asparagus Bundles 35
- Beef Curry 35
- Smothered Sirloin 36

CHAPTER 3: POULTRY RECIPES 37
- Chicken Nuggets 37
- Low-Carb Chicken Meatballs 37
- Buffalo Chicken Hot Wings 38
- Herb Chicken Thighs 39
- Lemon Pepper Chicken 39
- Mustard Honey Turkey Breast 40
- Air Fryer Chicken Cutlets 40
- Turkey Patties 41
- Rotisserie Chicken Fajitas 41
- Roasted Vegetable and Chicken Salad 42
- Crusted Chicken Drumsticks 43
- Thyme Turkey Breast 43
- Chicken Wings with Alfredo Sauce 44
- Chicken Drumsticks 45
- Chicken Schnitzel 45
- Chicken Rissoles 46
- Japanese Chicken Tenders 47
- Chicken Satay 47
- Greek Lemon Chicken 48
- Chicken Casserole 48
- Ranch Chicken Wings 49

- Chicken Mac and Cheese 50
- Broccoli Chicken Casserole 50
- Chicken Tikka Kebab 51

CHAPTER 4: VEGETABLES & SIDE DISHES 52

- Honey Brussels Sprouts 52
- Air Fried Tofu 52
- Roasted Bell Peppers 53
- Air Fried Pickles 53
- Zucchini Pizza 54
- Garlic-Roasted Bell Peppers 55
- Sweet Corn Fritters with Avocado 55
- Fried Green Beans with Pecorino Romano 56
- Corn on the Cob with Herb Butter 56
- Family Vegetable Gratin 57
- Crispy Tofu In Asian Sauce 58
- Crispy Blooming Onion 58
- Fried Okra 59
- Vegetarian Fajitas 60
- General Tso's Cauliflower 60
- Fried Peppers with Sriracha Mayo 61
- Classic Fried Pickles 62
- Tofu Tikka 62
- Spicy Glazed Carrots 63
- Rainbow Vegetable Fritters 64
- Balsamic Root Vegetables 64

CHAPTER 5: FISH AND SEAFOOD RECIPES 65

- Tomato Basil Scallops 65
- Shrimp Scampi 66
- Cilantro Lime Shrimps 66
- Breaded Sea Scallops 67
- Crumbed Fish 67
- Salmon Cakes with Sriracha Mayo 68
- Lemon Pepper Shrimp 69
- Lobster Tails with Garlic-Lemon Butter 69
- Coconut Shrimp 70
- Lemon Chili Salmon 70
- Tuna Burgers 71
- Breaded Cod 72
- Crab Stuffed Salmon 72
- Air Fried Salmon 73
- Crusted Mahi-Mahi 74
- Honey Tuna Steaks 74
- Salmon Cakes 75
- Crispy Fish Sticks 75
- Honey-Glazed Salmon 76

CHAPTER 6: SNACK RECIPES 77

- Zucchini Fries 77
- Avocado Fries 77
- Roasted Peanut Butter Squash 78
- Roasted Chickpeas 78
- Fried Spicy Green Beans 79
- Sweet Potato Nachos 79
- Rosemary-Garlic Brussels Sprouts 80
- Buffalo Cauliflower 81
- Mini Pizza 81
- Egg Rolls 82
- Fish & Chips 83
- Mozzarella Sticks 83
- Eggplant Fries 84
- Carrot Fries 84
- Kale Chips with Lemon Yogurt Sauce 85
- Basil Pesto Bruschetta 86
- Cinnamon Pear Chips 86
- Phyllo Vegetable Triangles 87

CHAPTER 7: DESSERTS RECIPES 88

- Chocolate Brownies 88
- Spiced Apples 88
- Sweet Potato Fries 89
- Chocolate Lava Cake 90
- Chocolate Donuts 90
- Peanut Butter Cookies 91
- Cheesecake Bites 92
- Chocolate Cake 92
- Grain-free Molten Lava Cakes 93
- Tahini-Crusted Chicken 94
- Oatmeal Chocolate Chunk Cookies 94
- Eggless & Vegan Air Fryer Cake 95
- Apple Cider Vinegar Donuts 95
- Molten Lava Mug Cake 96
- Coconut Flour Mug Cake 97

Mini Cheesecakes	98
Coconut Macaroons	98
Coconut Pie Air Fryer Recipe	99
Crustless Cheesecake	99
Low-Sugar Blueberry Cupcakes	100
Peach Cobbler	101
30 DAYS MEAL PLAN	102

INTRODUCTION

Welcome to our cookbook created especially for persons with diabetes! This cookbook provides a variety of tasty and healthful dishes geared to the nutritional demands of diabetics. We realize how difficult it is to manage diabetes, especially when it comes to selecting smart food choices that are both tasty and nutritious. Our cookbook is intended to give you with simple recipes that will help you maintain stable blood sugar levels while still enjoying a range of delicious and gratifying foods. The recipes in this cookbook have been carefully chosen and tested to guarantee that they are appropriate for diabetics. We've included recipes for breakfast, lunch, supper, snacks, and desserts, so you may eat a variety of foods throughout the day. Whether you've had diabetes for years or were just diagnosed, this cookbook is a great resource for anybody wanting to prepare nutritious and flavorful meals to help you manage your condition.

We understand that treating diabetes can be difficult, but that doesn't mean you have to sacrifice taste and flavor. We concentrated on utilizing clean, nutrient-dense foods in this cookbook to produce dishes that are not only healthful but also flavorful. We think that eating healthily should not be a work or a sacrifice, so we've compiled a list of simple dishes that you can enjoy at any time of day. Our meals, which range from substantial soups and stews to savory salads and stir-fries, are intended to be filling and nourishing. We've also included a range of dessert recipes so you can satisfy your sweet taste guilt-free. Our sweets are produced with natural sweeteners and ingredients with a low glycemic index, so they won't spike your blood sugar levels. Overall, this cookbook offers a complete guide to diabetes-friendly eating. It includes everything you need to prepare tasty and nutritious meals to help you manage your illness and enjoy a healthy, satisfying life. We hope you enjoy this cookbook and find it useful on your quest toward greater health.

UNDERSTANDING DIABETES

Diabetes affects nearly 30 million individuals in the United States, according to the Centers for Disease Control and Prevention (CDC). Surprisingly, one in every four of these people is unaware that they have this ailment. Diabetes is caused by the pancreas's inability to make or use insulin properly. Insulin is a hormone released by the pancreas into the circulation, where it is transported to cells. As sugar enters the cells, it is transformed into energy, which can be utilized immediately or stored for later use.

THE TWO TYPES OF DIABETES

Diabetes is classified into two types: type 1 and type 2.

Type 1 diabetes is an autoimmune illness in which the immune system targets and kills the pancreatic insulin-producing cells. As a result of little or no insulin production, patients with type 1 diabetes require insulin therapy for the rest of their lives. Type 1 diabetes is most commonly diagnosed in childhood or adolescence, although it can strike at any age.

Type 2 diabetes, on the other hand, is a metabolic illness that happens when the body develops insulin resistance or when the pancreas is unable to generate enough insulin to fulfill the body's demands. Obesity, physical inactivity, and a diet heavy in sugar and processed foods are all connected with type 2 diabetes. While type 2 diabetes may be controlled with lifestyle modifications including diet and exercise, some patients may need medication or insulin treatment.

Other kinds of diabetes, such as gestational diabetes (which develops during pregnancy) and monogenic diabetes, should be included (which is caused by a genetic mutation).

Type 1 diabetes, commonly known as insulin-dependent diabetes, is an autoimmune condition that affects around 10% of diabetics. It usually appears during childhood or adolescence, but it can appear at any age. The immune system targets and kills insulin-producing cells (beta cells) in the pancreas in type 1 diabetes. As a result of little or no insulin production, patients with type 1 diabetes require insulin therapy for the rest of their lives. Glucose (sugar) cannot enter the cells of the body to be used for energy unless insulin is present. This results in a buildup of glucose in the system, which can produce symptoms such as increased thirst and urination, impaired vision, exhaustion, and weight loss. Type 1 diabetes requires frequent blood sugar monitoring as well as regular insulin injections or the use of an insulin pump. It also entails careful nutrition and physical activity control to assist maintain stable blood sugar levels. While the precise etiology of type 1 diabetes is unknown, evidence indicates that both hereditary and environmental factors play a role in its development. Type 1 diabetes is not avoidable, and there is no treatment at the moment. Those with type 1 diabetes, on the other hand, can have healthy and meaningful lives with adequate care.

Type 2 diabetes is a metabolic condition that affects how insulin is used by the body to manage blood sugar (glucose) levels. In contrast to type 1 diabetes, the body still generates insulin in type 2 diabetes, but either not enough or the cells grow resistant to the effects of insulin. Type 2 diabetes is the most frequent kind, accounting for approximately 90-95% of all cases. It is most commonly diagnosed in middle-aged or elderly people, but it can occur at any age. Obesity, physical inactivity, a diet heavy in sugar and processed foods, and a family history of the illness are all risk factors for type 2 diabetes. Type 2 diabetes causes the body's cells to become insulin resistant, which means they don't respond as effectively to insulin's signals to absorb glucose from the blood. As a result, the pancreas produces extra insulin in an attempt to compensate. This can lead to a decline in insulin synthesis and subsequent blood sugar abnormalities over time. Increased thirst and urination, impaired vision, lethargy, and sluggish healing of wounds or sores are all symptoms of type 2 diabetes. Many persons with type 2 diabetes, on the other hand, have no symptoms and are not identified until regular blood tests indicate elevated blood sugar levels. To regulate blood sugar levels, type 2 diabetes requires lifestyle modifications such as diet and exercise, as well as medication in some circumstances. Insulin treatment may be required for certain persons with type 2 diabetes. While type 2 diabetes is mostly avoidable by lifestyle modifications, it is a chronic illness that must be managed on an ongoing basis. Type 2 diabetes, if not well managed, can lead to long-term problems such as cardiovascular disease, renal damage, and nerve damage.

HOW TO PREVENT IT?

There are various actions you may take to lower your chances of having type 2 diabetes, the most prevalent kind of diabetes:

Keep a healthy weight: Obesity and being overweight are key risk factors for type 2 diabetes. You may dramatically minimize your risk by decreasing weight and keeping a healthy weight.

Consume a well-balanced and nutritious diet: Concentrate on consuming nutritious grains, fruits and vegetables, and lean protein sources. Reduce your intake of saturated and trans fats, added sweets, and processed meals.

Obtain regular exercise: Strive for at least 30 minutes of moderate-intensity exercise most days of the week. This can include brisk walking, cycling, swimming, or any other activity that you love.

Don't smoke: Smoking raises the chance of acquiring type 2 diabetes as well as a number of other health issues. If you smoke, speak with your doctor about quitting methods.

Stress management: Persistent stress can raise the chance of developing type 2 diabetes, therefore learning appropriate stress management techniques is essential. Meditation, yoga, and deep breathing techniques are examples of such practices.

Frequent check-ups with your healthcare practitioner can help spot any possible health issues, such as type 2 diabetes, before they become more serious.

You may dramatically minimize your chance of getting type 2 diabetes and enhance your general health and well-being by implementing these lifestyle changes.

IS AIR FRYER GOOD FOR DIABETICS?

Cooking using an air fryer is a fantastic alternative for diabetics since it allows you to cook meals in a healthy manner by lowering the quantity of added fats and oils. Air fryers use hot air to cook food, resulting in a texture comparable to fried food without the extra oil and calories. This can be especially beneficial for diabetics who need to control their weight and blood sugar levels. Air fryers are not only a healthy cooking alternative, but they are also incredibly adaptable, since they can be used to cook a broad range of dishes, from chicken and fish to vegetables and even desserts. This can assist to keep meals interesting and reduce boredom from repeating dishes. But, keep in mind that the sort of food cooked in the air fryer is equally significant. If you cook unhealthy processed meals in the air fryer, it may not be advantageous to your diabetes control. It is critical to prepare nutrient-dense whole meals that are abundant in fiber, protein, and healthy fats. Therefore, using an air fryer as part of a balanced and nutritious diet can be a healthy and convenient alternative for those with diabetes.

RECIPES INDEX

A
Air Fried Pickles 53
Air Fried Salmon 73
Air Fried Tofu 52
Air Fryer Chicken Cutlets 40
Apple Cider Vinegar Donuts 95
Asparagus Omelet 18
Avocado Fries 77

B
Baked Eggs 18
Balsamic Root Vegetables 64
Banana Muffins 16
Basil Pesto Bruschetta 86
Beef Curry 35
Beef Korma Curry 28
Beef Schnitzel 33
Beef with Mushrooms 28
Breaded Cod 72
Breaded Sea Scallops 67

Breakfast Cheese Bread Cups 20
Breakfast Cookies 15
Broccoli Chicken Casserole 50
Buffalo Cauliflower 81
Buffalo Chicken Hot Wings 38

C
Carrot Fries 84
Cheeseburger Pockets 24
Cheesecake Bites 92
Chicken Casserole 48
Chicken Drumsticks 44
Chicken Mac and Cheese 50
Chicken Nuggets 37
Chicken Rissoles 46
Chicken Satay 47
Chicken Schnitzel 45
Chicken Tikka Kebab 51
Chicken Wings with Alfredo Sauce 44
Chocolate Brownies 88

Chocolate Cake 92
Chocolate Donuts 90
Chocolate Lava Cake 90
Cilantro Lime Shrimps 66
Cinnamon Pear Chips 86
Classic Fried Pickles 62
Coconut Flour Mug Cake 97
Coconut Macaroons 98
Coconut Pie Air Fryer Recipe 99
Coconut Shrimp 70
Corn on the Cob with Herb Butter 56
Crab Stuffed Salmon 72
Cracker Barrel Meatloaf 30
Crispy Blooming Onion 58
Crispy Empanadas 26
Crispy Fish Sticks 75
Crispy Tofu In Asian Sauce 58
Crumbed Fish 67
Crusted Chicken Drumsticks 43
Crusted Mahi-Mahi 74
Crustless Cheesecake 99

D
Diabetic-Friendly Meatballs 27
Diabetic-Friendly Meatloaf 34
Double Cheeseburger 33

E
Egg Bites 17
Egg Croquettes 15
Egg Rolls 82
Eggless & Vegan Air Fryer Cake 95
Eggplant Fries 84

F
Family Vegetable Gratin 57
Fish & Chips 83
Fried Egg 10
Fried Green Beans with Pecorino Romano 56
Fried Okra 59
Fried Peppers with Sriracha Mayo 61
Fried Spicy Green Beans 79

G
Garlic Butter Steaks 31
Garlic Rosemary Lamb Chops 22
Garlic-Roasted Bell Peppers 55
General Tso's Cauliflower 60
Grain-free Molten Lava Cakes 93
Greek Lemon Chicken 48
Grilled Cheese 12
Grilled Sandwich With Three Types Of Cheese 12

H
Hamburgers 25
Herb Chicken Thighs 38
Herb Frittata 11
Herbed Lamb Chops 21
Honey Brussels Sprouts 52
Honey Tuna Steaks 74
Honey-Glazed Salmon 76

I
Italian-Style Beef Meatballs 23

J
Japanese Chicken Tenders 47

K
Kale Chips with Lemon Yogurt Sauce 85

L
Lemon Chili Salmon 70
Lemon Greek Beef and Vegetables 29

Lemon Pepper Chicken 39
Lemon Pepper Shrimp 69
Lobster Tails with Garlic-Lemon Butter 69
Low-Carb Chicken Meatballs 37
Low-Fat Steak 27
Low-Sugar Blueberry Cupcakes 100

M
Meatloaf 24
Meatloaf Slider Wraps 32
Mini Cheesecakes 98
Mini Pizza 81
Molten Lava Mug Cake 96
Mongolian Beef Air Fryer Recipe 31
Morning Sausage Patties 17
Mozzarella Sticks 83
Mustard Honey Turkey Breast 40

O
Oatmeal Chocolate Chunk Cookies 94

P
Peach Cobbler 101
Peanut Butter Cookies 91
Phyllo Vegetable Triangles 87
Pumpkin Pie French Toast 19

R
Rainbow Vegetable Fritters 64
Ranch Chicken Wings 49
Roasted Bell Peppers 53
Roasted Chickpeas 78
Roasted Peanut Butter Squash 78
Roasted Vegetable and Chicken Salad 42
Rosemary-Garlic Brussels Sprouts 80
Rotisserie Chicken Fajitas 41

S
Salmon Cakes 75
Salmon Cakes with Sriracha Mayo 68
Santa Fe Style Pizza 14
Scallion Sandwich 13
Scrambled Egg 20
Shrimp Scampi 66
Smothered Sirloin 36
Spiced Apples 88
Spicy Glazed Carrots 63
Spicy Lamb Sirloin Steak 21
Spinach and Tomato Frittata 11
Steak Bites with Mushrooms 22
Steak with Asparagus Bundles 34
Steak Wrapped Asparagus 30
Sweet Corn Fritters with Avocado 55
Sweet Potato Fries 89
Sweet Potato Nachos 79

T
Tahini-Crusted Chicken 94
Tasty Chicken Patties 13
Thyme Turkey Breast 43
Tofu Scramble 10
Tofu Tikka 62
Tomato Basil Scallops 65
Tuna Burgers 71
Turkey Patties 41

V
Vegetarian Fajitas 60

Z
Zucchini Fries 77
Zucchini Pizza 54

CHAPTER 1: BREAKFAST RECIPES

Tofu Scramble

Prep Time: 10 minutes | **Cook Time:** 15 minutes | **Serve:** 2

Ingredients:
- 1 block of extra firm tofu
- 2 tablespoons olive oil
- 1/2 red bell pepper, diced
- 1/2 onion, diced
- 1/4 teaspoon garlic powder
- 1/4 teaspoon turmeric
- 1/4 teaspoon paprika
- Salt and pepper to taste

Directions:
1. Preheat air fryer to 375°F.
2. Drain and press the tofu to remove excess water.
3. Cut the tofu into cubes and place in a bowl.
4. Add olive oil, bell pepper, onion, garlic powder, turmeric, paprika, salt, and pepper. Mix until everything is evenly combined.
5. Place the tofu mixture in the air fryer basket and cook for 10 minutes.
6. Remove the basket and stir the tofu. Return to the air fryer and cook for an additional 5 minutes.

Nutrition: Calories: 160 | Total Fat: 10g | Saturated Fat: 1.5g | Cholesterol: 0mg | Sodium: 250mg | Carbohydrates: 8g | Fiber: 2g | Sugar: 3g | Protein: 10g

Fried Egg

Prep Time: 5 minutes | **Cook Time:** 10 minutes | **Serve:** 1

Ingredients:
1 egg
1 teaspoon olive oil
Salt and pepper to taste

Directions:
1. Preheat the air fryer to 350°F.
2. Grease the air fryer basket with the olive oil.
3. Crack the egg into the basket and season with salt and pepper.
4. Place the basket in the air fryer and cook for 10 minutes.

5. Remove the basket from the air fryer and serve.

Nutrition: Calories: 90 | Total Fat: 7g | Saturated Fat: 2g | Cholesterol: 186mg | Sodium: 77mg | Total Carbohydrate: 0g | Dietary Fiber: 0g | Sugars: 0g | Protein: 6g

Spinach and Tomato Frittata

Prep Time: 10 minutes | **Cook Time:** 20 minutes | **Serve:** 4

Ingredients:
- 2 tablespoons olive oil
- 1/2 cup diced onion
- 2 cloves garlic, minced
- 2 cups fresh spinach, chopped
- 1 cup cherry tomatoes, halved
- 8 large eggs
- 1/2 cup low-fat milk
- 1/2 teaspoon salt
- 1/4 teaspoon black pepper
- 1/4 cup shredded cheese

Directions:
1. Preheat the air fryer to 375°F.
2. Heat the olive oil in a large skillet over medium heat. Add the onion and garlic and cook until softened, about 5 minutes. Add the spinach and tomatoes and cook until the spinach is wilted and the tomatoes are softened, about 3 minutes.
3. In a large bowl, whisk together the eggs, milk, salt, and pepper. Add the cooked vegetables and stir to combine. Pour the mixture into the air fryer basket and cook for 15 minutes.
4. Sprinkle the cheese over the top and cook for an additional 5 minutes, or until the cheese is melted and the frittata is cooked through.

Nutrition: Calories: 181 | Total Fat: 11g | Saturated Fat: 3g | Cholesterol: 212mg | Sodium: 456mg | Carbohydrates: 8g | Fiber: 2g | Sugar: 4g | Protein: 12g

Herb Frittata

Prep Time: 10 minutes | **Cook Time:** 15 minutes | **Serve:** 4

Ingredients:
- 4 large eggs
- 2 tablespoons of skimmed milk
- 2 tablespoons of chopped fresh herbs (parsley, chives, basil, etc.)
- 2 tablespoons of grated Parmesan cheese
- 1/4 teaspoon of salt

- 1/4 teaspoon of ground black pepper
- 2 tablespoons of olive oil

Directions:
1. Preheat the air fryer to 400°F.
2. In a medium bowl, whisk together the eggs, milk, herbs, Parmesan cheese, salt, and pepper.
3. Grease the air fryer basket with the olive oil.
4. Pour the egg mixture into the air fryer basket.
5. Cook for 10 minutes or until the frittata is set.

Nutrition: Calories: 143 | Total Fat: 10g | Saturated Fat: 3g | Cholesterol: 186mg | Sodium: 253mg | Carbohydrates: 2g | Protein: 9g | Fiber: 0g

Grilled Cheese

Prep Time: 5 minutes | **Cook Time:** 10 minutes | **Serve:** 1

Ingredients:
2 slices of whole grain bread
1 tablespoon of low-fat butter
1 slice of reduced-fat cheese

Directions:
1. Preheat the air fryer to 350°F.
2. Spread butter on one side of each slice of bread.
3. Place the cheese slice between the two slices of bread.
4. Place the sandwich in the air fryer and cook for 5 minutes.
5. Flip the sandwich and cook for an additional 5 minutes.
6. Remove from the air fryer and enjoy.

Nutrition: Calories: 250 | Total Fat: 11g | Saturated Fat: 5g | Cholesterol: 20mg | Sodium: 470mg | Carbohydrates: 24g | Fiber: 4g | Sugar: 3g | Protein: 12g

Grilled Sandwich With Three Types Of Cheese

Prep Time: 10 minutes | **Cook Time:** 10 minutes | **Serve:** 2

Ingredients:
- 2 slices whole wheat bread
- 2 slices reduced fat cheddar cheese
- 2 slices reduced fat mozzarella cheese
- 2 slices reduced fat Swiss cheese
- 2 tablespoons olive oil
- 1 teaspoon garlic powder

- 1 teaspoon dried oregano

Directions:
1. Preheat air fryer to 350 degrees F.
2. Place bread slices in air fryer basket.
3. Drizzle olive oil over bread slices.
4. Sprinkle garlic powder and oregano over bread slices.
5. Place cheese slices on top of bread slices.
6. Close air fryer basket and cook for 10 minutes.

Nutrition: Calories: 320 | Fat: 15g | Carbohydrates: 28g | Protein: 18g

Tasty Chicken Patties

Prep Time: 10 minutes | **Cook Time:** 15 minutes | **Serve:** 4

Ingredients:
- 1 lb ground chicken
- 1/4 cup diced onion
- 1/4 cup diced bell pepper
- 1/4 cup diced celery
- 1/4 cup bread crumbs
- 1 teaspoon garlic powder
- 1 teaspoon onion powder
- 1 teaspoon paprika
- 1/2 teaspoon salt
- 1/2 teaspoon black pepper
- 2 tablespoons olive oil

Directions:
1. Preheat air fryer to 350 degrees F.
2. In a large bowl, combine ground chicken, onion, bell pepper, celery, bread crumbs, garlic powder, onion powder, paprika, salt, and black pepper. Mix until combined.
3. Form the mixture into 4 equal-sized patties.
4. Brush each patty with olive oil.
5. Place the patties in the air fryer and cook for 15 minutes, flipping halfway through.

Nutrition: Calories: 200 | Fat: 11g | Carbohydrates: 7g | Protein: 19g

Scallion Sandwich

Prep Time: 10 minutes | **Cook Time:** 10 minutes | **Serve:** 2

Ingredients:

- 2 slices of whole wheat bread
- 2 tablespoons of low-fat cream cheese
- 2 tablespoons of scallions, chopped
- 2 tablespoons of low-fat mayonnaise
- 1 teaspoon of olive oil
- Salt and pepper to taste

Directions:
1. Preheat the air fryer to 350°F.
2. Spread the cream cheese on one slice of bread.
3. Top with the scallions and the other slice of bread.
4. Brush the top of the sandwich with the olive oil.
5. Place the sandwich in the air fryer and cook for 5 minutes.
6. Flip the sandwich and cook for an additional 5 minutes.
7. Remove the sandwich from the air fryer and spread the mayonnaise on the top slice of bread.
8. Sprinkle with salt and pepper to taste.

Nutrition: Calories: 250 | Fat: 8g | Carbohydrates: 32g | Protein: 8g | Fiber: 4g

Santa Fe Style Pizza

Prep Time: 15 minutes | **Cook Time:** 15 minutes | **Serve:** 4

Ingredients:
- 2 cups cooked and shredded chicken
- 1/2 cup diced red onion
- 1/2 cup diced green bell pepper
- 1/2 cup diced red bell pepper
- 1/2 cup corn kernels
- 1/2 cup black beans
- 1/2 cup diced tomatoes
- 1/4 cup diced jalapenos
- 1/4 cup cilantro
- 1/4 cup olive oil
- 1/4 cup lime juice
- 1/4 cup taco seasoning
- 4 whole wheat tortillas
- 1/2 cup shredded cheese
- 1/4 cup sliced black olives

Directions:
1. Preheat the air fryer to 375 degrees Fahrenheit.

2. In a large bowl, combine the cooked chicken, red onion, bell peppers, corn, black beans, tomatoes, jalapenos, cilantro, olive oil, lime juice, and taco seasoning. Mix well until all ingredients are evenly distributed.
3. Place the tortillas on a cutting board and spread the chicken mixture evenly over the top. Sprinkle the cheese and black olives over the top.
4. Place the tortillas in the air fryer basket and cook for 8-10 minutes, or until the cheese is melted and the tortillas are lightly browned.
5. Remove from the air fryer and cut into slices. Serve warm.

Nutrition: Calories: 310 | Total Fat: 16g | Saturated Fat: 4g | Cholesterol: 45mg | Sodium: 740mg | Carbohydrates: 24g | Fiber: 5g | Sugar: 5g | Protein: 17g

Egg Croquettes

Prep Time: 10 minutes | **Cook Time:** 10 minutes | **Serve:** 4

Ingredients:
- 4 eggs
- 1/4 cup of grated cheese
- 1/4 cup of chopped parsley
- 1/4 cup of chopped onion
- 1/4 cup of breadcrumbs
- 1/4 teaspoon of garlic powder
- 1/4 teaspoon of paprika
- Salt and pepper to taste
- Olive oil spray

Directions:
1. Crack the eggs into a bowl and whisk until combined.
2. Add the cheese, parsley, onion, breadcrumbs, garlic powder, paprika, salt, and pepper and mix until combined.
3. Spray the air fryer basket with olive oil.
4. Divide the egg mixture into four equal parts and shape into patties.
5. Place the patties in the air fryer basket and cook for 10 minutes at 350°F.
6. Serve hot with your favorite side dish.

Nutrition: Calories: 200 | Fat: 10g | Carbohydrates: 14g | Protein: 12g | Fiber: 2g

Breakfast Cookies

Prep Time: 10 minutes | **Cook Time:** 10 minutes | **Serve:** 12

Ingredients:
1 cup rolled oats

1/2 cup almond flour
1/4 cup coconut sugar
1/4 cup almond butter
1/4 cup unsweetened applesauce
1/2 teaspoon baking powder
1/2 teaspoon ground cinnamon
1/4 teaspoon ground nutmeg
1/4 teaspoon salt
1/2 cup raisins

Directions:
1. Preheat the air fryer to 350°F.
2. In a medium bowl, combine the oats, almond flour, coconut sugar, almond butter, applesauce, baking powder, cinnamon, nutmeg, and salt. Mix until well combined.
3. Add the raisins and stir until evenly distributed.
4. Scoop the dough into 12 equal portions and shape into balls. Place the balls in the air fryer basket.
5. Cook for 10 minutes, shaking the basket halfway through.
6. Remove from the air fryer and let cool before serving.

Nutrition: Calories: 130 | Total Fat: 6g | Saturated Fat: 1g | Cholesterol: 0mg | Sodium: 80mg | Carbohydrates: 16g | Fiber: 2g | Sugar: 8g | Protein: 3g

Banana Muffins

Prep Time: 10 minutes | **Cook Time:** 15 minutes | **Serve:** 12 muffins

Ingredients:
- 2 cups all-purpose flour
- 1 teaspoon baking soda
- 1/2 teaspoon salt
- 1/2 cup granulated sugar
- 1/4 cup light brown sugar
- 1/2 cup unsalted butter, melted
- 2 large eggs
- 1 teaspoon vanilla extract
- 1/2 cup plain Greek yogurt
- 2 ripe bananas, mashed
- 1/2 cup chopped walnuts (optional)

Directions:
1. Preheat the air fryer to 350°F.
2. In a medium bowl, whisk together the flour, baking soda, and salt.
3. In a large bowl, mix together the sugars and melted butter until combined.
4. Add the eggs, vanilla extract, and Greek yogurt and mix until combined.

5. Add the mashed bananas and mix until combined.
6. Slowly add the dry ingredients to the wet ingredients and mix until just combined. Do not overmix.
7. Grease a 12-cup muffin tin with non-stick cooking spray.
8. Divide the batter evenly among the 12 muffin cups.
9. Place the muffin tin in the air fryer and cook for 15 minutes.
10. Allow the muffins to cool before serving.

Nutrition: Calories: 150 | Fat: 7g | Carbohydrates: 20g | Protein: 3g | Fiber: 1g | Sugar: 9g

Morning Sausage Patties

Prep Time: 10 minutes | **Cook Time:** 10 minutes | **Serve:** 4

Ingredients:
- 1 lb. ground turkey sausage
- 1/4 cup diced onion
- 1/4 cup diced bell pepper
- 1/4 teaspoon garlic powder
- 1/4 teaspoon black pepper
- 1/4 teaspoon dried oregano
- 1/4 teaspoon dried basil
- 1/4 teaspoon dried thyme
- 1/4 teaspoon red pepper flakes
- 1/4 teaspoon paprika
- 1/4 teaspoon sea salt
- 1 tablespoon olive oil

Directions:
1. Preheat the air fryer to 350°F.
2. In a large bowl, combine the ground turkey sausage, onion, bell pepper, garlic powder, black pepper, oregano, basil, thyme, red pepper flakes, paprika, and sea salt.
3. Mix until all ingredients are evenly distributed.
4. Form the mixture into 4 patties.
5. Brush the patties with olive oil.
6. Place the patties in the air fryer basket and cook for 10 minutes, flipping halfway through.

Nutrition: Calories: 260 | Total Fat: 17g | Saturated Fat: 5g | Cholesterol: 85mg | Sodium: 590mg | Carbohydrates: 3g | Fiber: 1g | Sugar: 1g | Protein: 24g

Egg Bites

Prep Time: 10 minutes | **Cook Time:** 15 minutes | **Serve:** 4

Ingredients:
- 4 large eggs
- 1/4 cup skim milk
- 1/4 cup shredded reduced-fat cheese
- 2 tablespoons chopped fresh herbs (such as parsley, chives, or basil)
- 1/4 teaspoon garlic powder
- Salt and pepper, to taste

Directions:
1. Preheat air fryer to 375 degrees F.
2. In a medium bowl, whisk together eggs, milk, cheese, herbs, garlic powder, salt, and pepper.
3. Grease four cups of a muffin tin with cooking spray.
4. Divide egg mixture evenly among the four cups.
5. Place muffin tin in air fryer and cook for 12-15 minutes, until eggs are set.

Nutrition: Calories: 92 | Fat: 5g | Protein: 7g | Carbs: 2g | Fiber: 0g | Sugar: 1g

Asparagus Omelet

Prep Time: 10 minutes | **Cook Time:** 10 minutes | **Serve:** 2

Ingredients:
- 2 tablespoons olive oil
- 2 cloves garlic, minced
- 1/2 cup chopped onion
- 1/2 cup chopped asparagus
- 4 large eggs
- 1/4 cup grated Parmesan cheese
- Salt and pepper to taste

Directions:
1. Preheat air fryer to 375°F.
2. Heat olive oil in a skillet over medium heat. Add garlic and onion and sauté until onion is softened, about 5 minutes. Add asparagus and cook for an additional 2 minutes.
3. In a medium bowl, whisk together eggs, Parmesan cheese, salt, and pepper. Add the cooked vegetables and mix until combined.
4. Grease the air fryer basket with cooking spray. Pour the egg mixture into the basket and spread evenly.
5. Cook for 10 minutes or until the omelet is cooked through.

Nutrition: Calories: 203 | Fat: 14 g | Protein: 11 g | Carbs: 6 g | Fiber: 2 g | Sodium: 245 mg

Baked Eggs

Prep Time: 5 minutes | **Cook Time:** 10 minutes | **Serve:** 2

Ingredients:
- 2 eggs
- 2 tablespoons of low-fat milk
- 1 teaspoon of olive oil
- Salt and pepper to taste
- 1/4 cup of shredded cheese

Directions:
1. Preheat the air fryer to 350 degrees Fahrenheit.
2. In a small bowl, whisk together the eggs, milk, olive oil, salt, and pepper.
3. Grease the air fryer basket with cooking spray.
4. Pour the egg mixture into the air fryer basket.
5. Sprinkle the shredded cheese over the eggs.
6. Cook for 10 minutes, or until the eggs are cooked through.

Nutrition: Calories: 150 | Fat: 10g | Protein: 11g | Carbohydrates: 2g | Fiber: 0g | Sodium: 200mg

Pumpkin Pie French Toast

Prep Time: 10 minutes | **Cook Time:** 15 minutes | **Serve:** 4

Ingredients:
- 8 slices of whole wheat bread
- 1/2 cup canned pumpkin puree
- 2 eggs
- 1/4 cup almond milk
- 1 teaspoon ground cinnamon
- 1/2 teaspoon ground nutmeg
- 1/4 teaspoon ground ginger
- 1/4 teaspoon ground allspice
- 1 tablespoon maple syrup
- 1 tablespoon coconut oil
- 2 tablespoons chopped pecans
- 2 tablespoons raisins
- Non-stick cooking spray

Directions:
1. Preheat the air fryer to 375 degrees F.

2. In a large bowl, whisk together the pumpkin puree, eggs, almond milk, cinnamon, nutmeg, ginger, allspice, and maple syrup.
3. Dip each slice of bread into the pumpkin mixture, coating both sides.
4. Place the slices of bread in the air fryer basket.
5. Spray the top of the bread with non-stick cooking spray.
6. Cook for 8 minutes, flipping the bread halfway through.
7. Remove from the air fryer and top with the pecans and raisins.
8. Drizzle with the coconut oil and serve.

Nutrition: Calories: 250 | Fat: 8g | Carbohydrates: 36g | Protein: 8g | Sodium: 250mg | Fiber: 4g

Scrambled Egg

Prep Time: 5 minutes | **Cook Time:** 10 minutes | **Serve:** 2

Ingredients:
- 4 large eggs
- 2 tablespoons of skim milk
- 2 tablespoons of olive oil
- 1/2 teaspoon of salt
- 1/4 teaspoon of ground black pepper
- 2 tablespoons of shredded cheese (optional)

Directions:
1. Preheat the air fryer to 350 degrees F.
2. In a medium bowl, whisk together the eggs, milk, olive oil, salt, and pepper.
3. Pour the egg mixture into the air fryer basket and spread it out evenly.
4. Cook for 10 minutes, stirring occasionally.
5. Add the cheese (optional) and cook for an additional 2 minutes.

Nutrition: Calories: 190 | Fat: 13g | Protein: 12g | Carbs: 2g | Fiber: 0g | Sodium: 400mg

Breakfast Cheese Bread Cups

Prep Time: 10 minutes | **Cook Time:** 15 minutes | **Serve:** 6

Ingredients:
- 2 cups whole wheat flour
- 1 teaspoon baking powder
- 1/2 teaspoon baking soda
- 1/2 teaspoon salt
- 1/4 cup olive oil
- 1/2 cup low-fat buttermilk
- 1/2 cup shredded reduced-fat cheddar cheese

- 1/4 cup chopped fresh chives
- 1/4 cup chopped fresh parsley

Directions:
1. Preheat the air fryer to 375°F.
2. In a medium bowl, whisk together the flour, baking powder, baking soda, and salt.
3. In a separate bowl, whisk together the olive oil and buttermilk.
4. Add the wet ingredients to the dry ingredients and stir until just combined.
5. Fold in the cheese, chives, and parsley.
6. Grease a 6-cup muffin tin with cooking spray. Divide the batter evenly among the muffin cups.
7. Place the muffin tin in the air fryer and cook for 15 minutes, or until golden brown.

Nutrition: Calories: 150 | Fat: 7g | Carbohydrates: 16g | Protein: 5g | Sodium: 300mg | Fiber: 2g

CHAPTER 2: MEAT RECIPES

Herbed Lamb Chops

Prep Time: 10 minutes | **Cook Time:** 15 minutes | Serves: 4

Ingredients:
4 lamb chops
1 tablespoon olive oil
1 teaspoon dried oregano
1 teaspoon dried thyme
1 teaspoon garlic powder
1 teaspoon onion powder
Salt and pepper to taste

Directions:
1. Preheat the air fryer to 375°F.
2. In a small bowl, mix together the oregano, thyme, garlic powder, onion powder, salt, and pepper.
3. Rub the lamb chops with the olive oil and then sprinkle the herb mixture over them.
4. Place the lamb chops in the air fryer basket and cook for 10 minutes.
5. Flip the lamb chops over and cook for an additional 5 minutes.

Nutrition: Calories: 220 | Fat: 13g | Protein: 23g | Carbohydrates: 0g | Fiber: 0g | Sodium: 150mg

Spicy Lamb Sirloin Steak

Prep Time: 10 minutes | **Cook Time:** 15 minutes | Serves: 4

Ingredients:

- 4 lamb sirloin steaks
- 2 tablespoons olive oil
- 2 tablespoons chili powder
- 1 teaspoon garlic powder
- 1 teaspoon onion powder
- 1 teaspoon paprika
- 1 teaspoon cumin
- 1 teaspoon oregano
- 1 teaspoon salt
- 1 teaspoon black pepper

Directions:
1. Preheat the air fryer to 400°F.
2. In a small bowl, mix together the chili powder, garlic powder, onion powder, paprika, cumin, oregano, salt, and pepper.
3. Rub the olive oil onto both sides of the steaks.
4. Sprinkle the spice mixture onto both sides of the steaks.
5. Place the steaks in the air fryer and cook for 10-15 minutes, flipping halfway through.

Nutrition: Calories: 250 | Total Fat: 15g | Saturated Fat: 4g | Cholesterol: 70mg | Sodium: 500mg | Carbohydrates: 2g | Protein: 25g

Garlic Rosemary Lamb Chops

Prep Time: 10 minutes | **Cook Time:** 15 minutes | **Serve:** 4

Ingredients:
- 8 lamb chops
- 2 cloves garlic, minced
- 2 tablespoons olive oil
- 2 tablespoons fresh rosemary, chopped
- Salt and pepper to taste

Directions:
1. Preheat air fryer to 400°F.
2. In a small bowl, combine garlic, olive oil, rosemary, salt and pepper. Mix until combined.
3. Place lamb chops in a shallow dish and pour garlic mixture over the chops. Rub the mixture into the chops until evenly coated.
4. Place the lamb chops in the air fryer basket and cook for 10-15 minutes, flipping once halfway through.

Nutrition: Calories: 280 | Total Fat: 16g | Saturated Fat: 5g | Cholesterol: 85mg | Sodium: 150mg | Carbohydrates: 1g | Protein: 28g

Steak Bites with Mushrooms

Prep Time: 10 minutes | **Cook Time:** 15 minutes | Serves: 4

Ingredients:
-1 lb sirloin steak, cut into 1-inch cubes
-1/2 cup mushrooms, sliced
-1/4 cup olive oil
-1 teaspoon garlic powder
-1 teaspoon onion powder
-1 teaspoon paprika
-1/2 teaspoon salt
-1/4 teaspoon black pepper

Directions:
1. Preheat the air fryer to 400°F.
2. In a large bowl, combine the steak cubes, mushrooms, olive oil, garlic powder, onion powder, paprika, salt, and pepper. Mix until the steak and mushrooms are evenly coated.
3. Place the steak and mushrooms in the air fryer basket. Cook for 8 minutes.
4. Remove the basket from the air fryer and shake the steak and mushrooms. Return the basket to the air fryer and cook for an additional 7 minutes.
5. Serve the steak bites with mushrooms.

Nutrition: Calories: 270 | Fat: 18 g | Protein: 24 g | Carbohydrates: 3 g | Fiber: 1 g | Sodium: 590 mg

Italian-Style Beef Meatballs

Prep Time: 10 minutes | **Cook Time:** 20 minutes | **Serve:** 4

Ingredients:
- 1 lb lean ground beef
- 2 cloves garlic, minced
- 1/4 cup grated Parmesan cheese
- 1/4 cup chopped fresh parsley
- 1/4 cup Italian-style breadcrumbs
- 1 large egg, lightly beaten
- 1/2 teaspoon salt
- 1/4 teaspoon black pepper
- 2 tablespoons olive oil

Directions:
1. Preheat air fryer to 375°F.

2. In a large bowl, combine ground beef, garlic, Parmesan cheese, parsley, breadcrumbs, egg, salt, and pepper. Mix until combined.
3. Form into 1-inch meatballs and place in air fryer basket.
4. Drizzle with olive oil.
5. Cook for 10 minutes, shaking basket halfway through.
6. Increase temperature to 400°F and cook for an additional 10 minutes, shaking basket halfway through.

Nutrition: Calories: 250 | Total Fat: 14g | Saturated Fat: 4g | Cholesterol: 85mg | Sodium: 450mg | Carbohydrates: 8g | Fiber: 1g | Sugar: 1g | Protein: 22g

Meatloaf

Prep Time: 10 minutes | **Cook Time:** 20 minutes | **Serve:** 6

Ingredients:
1 lb. lean ground beef
1/2 cup diced onion
1/2 cup diced bell pepper
1/2 cup diced celery
1/2 cup low-fat milk
1/2 cup rolled oats
1/4 cup grated Parmesan cheese
1 egg, lightly beaten
1 teaspoon garlic powder
1 teaspoon onion powder
1 teaspoon dried oregano
1 teaspoon dried basil
1/2 teaspoon salt
1/4 teaspoon ground black pepper

Directions:
1. Preheat air fryer to 375°F.
2. In a large bowl, combine ground beef, onion, bell pepper, celery, milk, oats, Parmesan cheese, egg, garlic powder, onion powder, oregano, basil, salt, and pepper. Mix until all ingredients are well blended.
3. Form mixture into a loaf shape and place in the air fryer basket.
4. Cook for 15 minutes.
5. Carefully flip the meatloaf over and cook for an additional 5 minutes.
6. Remove from air fryer and let cool for 5 minutes before serving.

Nutrition: Calories: 180 | Fat: 7g | Carbohydrates: 9g | Protein: 19g | Sodium: 375mg | Fiber: 2g

Cheeseburger Pockets

Prep Time: 10 minutes | **Cook Time:** 15 minutes | **Serve:** 4

Ingredients:
- 1 lb lean ground beef
- 1/2 cup diced onion
- 1/2 cup diced bell pepper
- 1 teaspoon garlic powder
- 1 teaspoon onion powder
- 1 teaspoon Worcestershire sauce
- 1/2 teaspoon salt
- 1/4 teaspoon black pepper
- 1/2 cup shredded low-fat cheddar cheese
- 4 whole-wheat pita pockets
- Non-stick cooking spray

Directions:
1. Preheat air fryer to 375°F.
2. In a large bowl, combine ground beef, onion, bell pepper, garlic powder, onion powder, Worcestershire sauce, salt, and black pepper. Mix until all ingredients are evenly distributed.
3. Divide the mixture into four equal portions and shape each portion into a patty.
4. Place the patties in the air fryer basket and cook for 8 minutes.
5. Flip the patties and cook for an additional 7 minutes.
6. Place the cooked patties on the bottom half of each pita pocket. Top each patty with 1 tablespoon of shredded cheese.
7. Spray the top of each pita pocket with non-stick cooking spray and place in the air fryer. Cook for 2 minutes.
8. Remove from the air fryer and top each pocket with the remaining half of the pita pocket. Serve.

Nutrition: Calories: 327 | Fat: 13g | Protein: 24g | Carbohydrates: 24g | Fiber: 4g | Sodium: 545mg

Hamburgers

Prep Time: 10 minutes | **Cook Time:** 15 minutes | **Serve:** 4

Ingredients:
- 1 lb. lean ground beef
- 4 whole wheat hamburger buns
- 1/4 cup diced onion
- 1/4 cup diced bell pepper
- 1/4 cup diced mushrooms
- 1/4 cup grated low-fat cheese
- 1 teaspoon garlic powder

- 1 teaspoon onion powder
- 1 teaspoon black pepper
- 1 teaspoon Worcestershire sauce
- Salt to taste

Directions:
1. Preheat air fryer to 375°F.
2. In a large bowl, mix together ground beef, onion, bell pepper, mushrooms, cheese, garlic powder, onion powder, black pepper, Worcestershire sauce, and salt.
3. Form the mixture into 4 equal-sized patties.
4. Place the patties in the air fryer basket and cook for 8 minutes.
5. Flip the patties and cook for an additional 7 minutes.
6. Serve on whole wheat hamburger buns.

Nutrition: Calories: 240 | Total Fat: 9g | Saturated Fat: 4g | Cholesterol: 55mg | Sodium: 240mg | Carbohydrates: 21g | Fiber: 3g | Protein: 19g

Crispy Empanadas

Prep Time: 15 minutes | **Cook Time:** 15 minutes | **Serve:** 8

Ingredients:
-1 package of low-carb empanada wrappers
-1/2 cup of cooked chicken, shredded
-1/2 cup of cooked black beans
-1/2 cup of cooked corn
-1/4 cup of diced red bell pepper
-1/4 cup of diced onion
-1/4 cup of shredded cheese
-1 teaspoon of chili powder
-1 teaspoon of cumin
-1/2 teaspoon of garlic powder
-1/4 teaspoon of salt
-1/4 teaspoon of black pepper
-1/4 cup of olive oil

Directions:
1. Preheat the air fryer to 350 degrees F.
2. In a medium bowl, combine the chicken, black beans, corn, bell pepper, onion, cheese, chili powder, cumin, garlic powder, salt, and black pepper. Mix until all ingredients are evenly distributed.
3. Place one empanada wrapper on a flat surface. Place 2 tablespoons of the filling in the center of the wrapper. Fold the wrapper in half and press the edges together to seal. Repeat with the remaining wrappers and filling.

4. Brush the empanadas with olive oil. Place the empanadas in the air fryer and cook for 15 minutes, flipping halfway through.

Nutrition: Calories: 140 | Fat: 7g | Carbohydrates: 11g | Protein: 8g | Sodium: 200mg

Diabetic-Friendly Meatballs

Prep Time: 10 minutes | **Cook Time:** 10 minutes | **Serve:** 4

Ingredients:
1 lb. lean ground beef
1/2 cup oat bran
1/4 cup grated Parmesan cheese
1/4 cup minced onion
2 cloves garlic, minced
1 teaspoon Italian seasoning
1/2 teaspoon salt
1/4 teaspoon black pepper
1/4 teaspoon red pepper flakes
1 egg
1 tablespoon olive oil

Directions:
1. In a large bowl, combine the ground beef, oat bran, Parmesan cheese, onion, garlic, Italian seasoning, salt, black pepper, red pepper flakes, and egg. Mix until all ingredients are evenly combined.
2. Use your hands to form the mixture into 1-inch meatballs.
3. Place the meatballs in the air fryer and drizzle with the olive oil.
4. Cook the meatballs in the air fryer at 400°F for 10 minutes, or until the meatballs are cooked through.

Nutrition: Calories: 180 | Total Fat: 9g | Saturated Fat: 3g | Trans Fat: 0g | Cholesterol: 70mg | Sodium: 320mg | Carbohydrates: 6g | Fiber: 2g | Sugar: 1g | Protein: 18g

Low-Fat Steak

Prep Time: 10 minutes | **Cook Time:** 15 minutes | **Serve:** 4

Ingredients:
- 4 (4-ounce) lean steaks
- 1 tablespoon olive oil
- 1 teaspoon garlic powder
- 1 teaspoon onion powder
- 1 teaspoon paprika

- 1 teaspoon dried oregano
- 1 teaspoon dried thyme
- Salt and pepper to taste

Directions:
1. Preheat air fryer to 400°F.
2. Rub steaks with olive oil and season with garlic powder, onion powder, paprika, oregano, thyme, salt, and pepper.
3. Place steaks in air fryer and cook for 8 minutes. Flip steaks and cook for an additional 7 minutes or until desired doneness.
4. Remove steaks from air fryer and let rest for 5 minutes before serving.
5. Serve with your favorite sides and enjoy!
6. Store leftovers in an airtight container in the refrigerator for up to 3 days.

Nutrition: Calories: 150 | Fat: 6g | Carbohydrates: 0g | Protein: 22g

Beef with Mushrooms

Prep Time: 10 minutes | **Cook Time:** 20 minutes | **Serve:** 4

Ingredients:
- 1 lb lean ground beef
- 1/2 cup diced onion
- 8 ounces mushrooms, sliced
- 1/4 teaspoon garlic powder
- 1/4 teaspoon onion powder
- 1/4 teaspoon black pepper
- 1/2 teaspoon salt
- 2 tablespoons olive oil

Directions:
1. Preheat the air fryer to 350°F.
2. In a large bowl, combine the ground beef, onion, mushrooms, garlic powder, onion powder, black pepper, and salt. Mix until all ingredients are evenly distributed.
3. Form the mixture into 4 patties.
4. Place the patties in the air fryer basket and drizzle with olive oil.
5. Cook for 15 minutes, flipping the patties halfway through.
6. Serve with your favorite sides.

Nutrition: Calories: 250 | Total Fat: 13g | Saturated Fat: 4g | Cholesterol: 55mg | Sodium: 420mg | Carbohydrates: 6g | Fiber: 1g | Protein: 23g

Beef Korma Curry

Prep Time: 10 minutes | **Cook Time:** 30 minutes | Serves: 4

Ingredients:
1 lb lean ground beef
1 onion, diced
2 cloves garlic, minced
1 teaspoon ground ginger
1 teaspoon ground cumin
1 teaspoon ground coriander
1 teaspoon garam masala
1 teaspoon turmeric
1 teaspoon chili powder
1 teaspoon salt
1 (14.5 ounce) can diced tomatoes
1 (14.5 ounce) can light coconut milk
1/4 cup fresh cilantro, chopped

Directions:
1. Preheat the air fryer to 375°F.
2. In a large bowl, combine the ground beef, onion, garlic, ginger, cumin, coriander, garam masala, turmeric, chili powder, and salt. Mix until combined.
3. Place the beef mixture in the air fryer basket and cook for 10 minutes, stirring occasionally.
4. Add the diced tomatoes and coconut milk and stir to combine. Cook for an additional 10 minutes, stirring occasionally.
5. Add the cilantro and stir to combine. Cook for an additional 10 minutes, stirring occasionally.

Nutrition: Calories: 270 | Total Fat: 14g | Saturated Fat: 8g | Cholesterol: 55mg | Sodium: 590mg | Carbohydrates: 12g | Fiber: 2g | Sugar: 4g | Protein: 22g

Lemon Greek Beef and Vegetables

Prep Time: 10 minutes | **Cook Time:** 20 minutes | Serves: 4

Ingredients:
1 lb lean ground beef
1/2 cup diced onion
1/2 cup diced bell pepper
1/2 cup diced celery
1/2 cup diced carrots
1/2 cup diced zucchini
1/4 cup diced tomatoes
1/4 cup lemon juice

1/4 cup olive oil
1 tsp garlic powder
1 tsp oregano
1/2 tsp salt
1/4 tsp black pepper

Directions:
1. Preheat air fryer to 375°F.
2. In a large bowl, combine ground beef, onion, bell pepper, celery, carrots, zucchini, tomatoes, lemon juice, olive oil, garlic powder, oregano, salt and pepper. Mix until all ingredients are evenly distributed.
3. Place mixture in air fryer basket and cook for 15 minutes.
4. After 15 minutes, remove basket from air fryer and stir. Place back in air fryer and cook for an additional 5 minutes.

Nutrition: Calories: 250 | Total Fat: 15g | Saturated Fat: 4g | Cholesterol: 55mg | Sodium: 300mg | Carbohydrates: 8g | Fiber: 2g | Sugar: 3g | Protein: 19g

Cracker Barrel Meatloaf

Prep Time: 10 minutes | **Cook Time:** 25 minutes | **Serve:** 4

Ingredients:
- 1 lb. ground beef
- 1/2 cup crushed crackers (low sodium)
- 1/4 cup diced onion
- 1/4 cup diced bell pepper
- 1/4 cup diced celery
- 1/2 teaspoon garlic powder
- 1/2 teaspoon black pepper
- 1/2 teaspoon dried oregano
- 1/2 teaspoon dried thyme
- 1/2 teaspoon dried basil
- 1/4 cup ketchup
- 1 egg, lightly beaten
- 2 tablespoons Worcestershire sauce

Directions:
1. Preheat air fryer to 375°F.
2. In a large bowl, combine all ingredients. Mix well.
3. Form the mixture into a loaf shape and place in the air fryer basket.
4. Cook for 25 minutes, flipping halfway through.
5. Serve with your favorite side dishes.

Nutrition: Calories: 310 | Total Fat: 15g | Saturated Fat: 6g | Cholesterol: 110mg | Sodium: 320mg | Carbohydrates: 15g | Fiber: 1g | Sugar: 4g | Protein: 24g

Steak Wrapped Asparagus

Prep Time: 10 minutes | **Cook Time:** 15 minutes | Serves: 4

Ingredients:
- 4 thin-cut steaks
- 8 asparagus spears
- 2 tablespoons olive oil
- Salt and pepper to taste
- 2 tablespoons grated Parmesan cheese

Directions:
1. Preheat the air fryer to 400 degrees F.
2. Place the steaks on a cutting board and season with salt and pepper.
3. Place two asparagus spears on each steak and roll up. Secure with toothpicks.
4. Brush the steak rolls with olive oil and sprinkle with Parmesan cheese.
5. Place the steak rolls in the air fryer basket and cook for 15 minutes, flipping halfway through.

Nutrition: Calories: 300 | Fat: 16g | Protein: 28g | Carbs: 4g | Fiber: 2g | Sodium: 200mg

Garlic Butter Steaks

Prep Time: 10 minutes | **Cook Time:** 15 minutes | **Serve:** 4

Ingredients:
- 4 steaks of your choice
- 2 tablespoons of garlic butter
- 2 tablespoons of olive oil
- Salt and pepper to taste

Directions:
1. Preheat the air fryer to 375°F.
2. Rub the steaks with olive oil and season with salt and pepper.
3. Place the steaks in the air fryer and cook for 10 minutes.
4. Flip the steaks and spread the garlic butter on top.
5. Cook for an additional 5 minutes or until the steaks reach the desired doneness.

Nutrition: Calories: 300 | Fat: 20g | Protein: 25g | Carbs: 2g | Fiber: 0g

Mongolian Beef Air Fryer Recipe

Prep Time: 10 minutes | **Cook Time:** 15 minutes | **Serve:** 4

Ingredients:
- 1 lb flank steak, thinly sliced
- 2 tablespoons low-sodium soy sauce
- 2 tablespoons cornstarch
- 2 tablespoons olive oil
- 1 teaspoon garlic, minced
- 1 teaspoon fresh ginger, minced
- 1/4 cup low-sodium beef broth
- 2 tablespoons hoisin sauce
- 2 tablespoons rice vinegar
- 2 tablespoons green onions, chopped
- 1/4 teaspoon red pepper flakes

Directions:
1. Place the steak in a bowl and add the soy sauce and cornstarch. Toss to coat the steak and set aside.
2. Heat the oil in the air fryer and add the garlic and ginger. Cook for 1 minute.
3. Add the steak and cook for 5 minutes, stirring occasionally.
4. Add the beef broth, hoisin sauce, rice vinegar, green onions, and red pepper flakes. Stir to combine.
5. Cook for an additional 5 minutes, stirring occasionally.
6. Serve over steamed rice or vegetables.

Nutrition: Calories: 200 | Fat: 8g | Carbohydrates: 10g | Protein: 22g

Meatloaf Slider Wraps

Prep Time: 10 minutes | **Cook Time:** 15 minutes | **Serve:** 4

Ingredients:
- 1 lb. ground beef (90/10)
- 1/4 cup diced onion
- 1/4 cup diced bell pepper
- 1/4 cup diced celery
- 1/4 cup low sodium ketchup
- 1/4 cup low sodium Worcestershire sauce
- 1/4 cup low sodium barbecue sauce
- 2 tablespoons Dijon mustard
- 1/4 cup rolled oats
- 2 tablespoons chopped parsley
- 2 tablespoons chopped basil
- 4 whole wheat wraps
- 2 tablespoons olive oil

Directions:
1. Preheat air fryer to 375°F.
2. In a large bowl, combine ground beef, onion, bell pepper, celery, ketchup, Worcestershire sauce, barbecue sauce, Dijon mustard, rolled oats, parsley, and basil. Mix until all ingredients are evenly distributed.
3. Divide the mixture into 4 equal portions and shape each portion into a patty. Place the patties in the air fryer and cook for 10 minutes.
4. Remove the patties from the air fryer and place them on the wraps. Drizzle with olive oil and wrap up.
5. Place the wraps in the air fryer and cook for an additional 5 minutes.

Nutrition: Calories: 519 | Total Fat: 22g | Saturated Fat: 8g | Cholesterol: 82mg | Sodium: 667mg | Carbohydrates: 45g | Fiber: 5g | Sugar: 12g | Protein: 33g

Double Cheeseburger

Prep Time: 10 minutes | **Cook Time:** 15 minutes | **Serve:** 2

Ingredients:
- 2 whole wheat hamburger buns
- 2 lean ground beef patties
- 2 slices of reduced fat cheese
- 2 tablespoons of ketchup
- 2 tablespoons of mustard
- 2 tablespoons of diced onions
- 2 tablespoons of diced tomatoes
- Salt and pepper to taste

Directions:
1. Preheat the air fryer to 375 degrees F.
2. Place the ground beef patties in the air fryer and cook for 10 minutes, flipping halfway through.
3. Place the buns in the air fryer and cook for 2 minutes.
4. Place the patties on the buns and top with cheese, ketchup, mustard, onions, and tomatoes.
5. Place the burgers back in the air fryer and cook for an additional 3 minutes.
6. Remove from the air fryer and serve.

Nutrition: Calories: 300 | Fat: 12g | Carbohydrates: 25g | Protein: 25g

Beef Schnitzel

Prep Time: 10 minutes | **Cook Time:** 10 minutes | **Serve:** 4

Ingredients:

- 4 boneless beef schnitzel cutlets
- 2 tablespoons olive oil
- 1 teaspoon garlic powder
- 1 teaspoon onion powder
- 1 teaspoon paprika
- 1 teaspoon dried oregano
- 1 teaspoon dried parsley
- Salt and pepper to taste

Directions:
1. Preheat the air fryer to 400°F.
2. In a shallow bowl, combine the olive oil, garlic powder, onion powder, paprika, oregano, parsley, salt, and pepper. Mix until combined.
3. Dip each schnitzel cutlet into the mixture, coating both sides.
4. Place the schnitzel cutlets in the air fryer basket.
5. Cook for 5 minutes, then flip the schnitzel cutlets and cook for an additional 5 minutes.
6. Serve with your favorite side dishes.

Nutrition: Calories: 200 | Fat: 11g | Carbohydrates: 0g | Protein: 22g

Diabetic-Friendly Meatloaf

Prep Time: 10 minutes | **Cook Time:** 25 minutes | **Serve:** 4-6

Ingredients:
1 lb. lean ground beef
1/2 cup finely chopped onion
1/2 cup finely chopped bell pepper
1/2 cup finely chopped mushrooms
1/2 cup quick-cooking oats
1/4 cup low-sodium ketchup
1/4 cup low-fat milk
1 egg, lightly beaten
1/2 teaspoon garlic powder
1/2 teaspoon onion powder
1/4 teaspoon black pepper

Directions:
1. Preheat the air fryer to 375°F.
2. In a large bowl, combine the ground beef, onion, bell pepper, mushrooms, oats, ketchup, milk, egg, garlic powder, onion powder, and black pepper. Mix until all ingredients are evenly distributed.
3. Form the mixture into a loaf shape and place it in the air fryer basket.
4. Cook the meatloaf for 25 minutes, flipping it halfway through.
5. Remove the meatloaf from the air fryer and let it rest for 5 minutes before slicing and serving.

Nutrition: Calories: 215 | Fat: 8g | Carbohydrates: 12g | Protein: 22g | Sodium: 170mg | Fiber: 2g

Steak with Asparagus Bundles

Prep Time: 10 minutes | **Cook Time:** 15 minutes | Serves: 4

Ingredients:
- 4 (4-ounce) sirloin steaks
- 1/4 teaspoon garlic powder
- 1/4 teaspoon onion powder
- 1/4 teaspoon black pepper
- 2 tablespoons olive oil
- 8 asparagus spears, trimmed
- 4 slices reduced-fat Swiss cheese
- 2 tablespoons reduced-fat butter
- 2 tablespoons freshly squeezed lemon juice
- 2 tablespoons chopped fresh parsley

Directions:
1. Preheat the air fryer to 400°F.
2. Season the steaks with garlic powder, onion powder, and black pepper. Drizzle with olive oil.
3. Place the steaks in the air fryer basket and cook for 8 minutes. Flip the steaks and cook for an additional 5 minutes.
4. Meanwhile, wrap 2 asparagus spears in each slice of cheese. Place the bundles in the air fryer basket and cook for 5 minutes.
5. In a small saucepan, melt the butter and lemon juice over medium heat. Stir in the parsley.
6. Serve the steaks and asparagus bundles with the lemon butter sauce.

Nutrition: Calories: 437 | Fat: 24g | Protein: 39g | Carbohydrates: 7g | Fiber: 2g | Sodium: 528mg

Beef Curry

Prep Time: 10 minutes | **Cook Time:** 20 minutes | **Serve:** 4

Ingredients:
- 2 tablespoons olive oil
- 1 onion, diced
- 2 cloves garlic, minced
- 1 teaspoon ground ginger
- 1 teaspoon ground cumin
- 1 teaspoon ground coriander
- 1 teaspoon ground turmeric
- 1 teaspoon garam masala

- 1/2 teaspoon chili powder
- 1/4 teaspoon ground cinnamon
- 1/4 teaspoon ground cardamom
- 1 pound lean ground beef
- 1 (14.5 ounce) can diced tomatoes, undrained
- 1 (14.5 ounce) can light coconut milk
- 1/4 cup chopped fresh cilantro
- Salt and pepper to taste

Directions:
1. Preheat the air fryer to 375 degrees F.
2. Heat the olive oil in a large skillet over medium heat. Add the onion and garlic and cook until softened, about 5 minutes.
3. Add the ginger, cumin, coriander, turmeric, garam masala, chili powder, cinnamon, and cardamom and cook for 1 minute.
4. Add the ground beef and cook until browned, about 5 minutes.
5. Add the diced tomatoes and coconut milk and bring to a simmer. Simmer for 10 minutes.
6. Transfer the beef curry to the air fryer basket and cook for 10 minutes.
7. Serve the beef curry with cilantro and salt and pepper to taste.

Nutrition: Calories: 310 | Fat: 17g | Saturated Fat: 8g | Cholesterol: 60mg | Sodium: 250mg | Carbohydrates: 14g | Fiber: 2g | Sugar: 5g | Protein: 24g

Smothered Sirloin

Prep Time: 10 minutes | **Cook Time:** 15 minutes | **Serve:** 4

Ingredients:
1 lb sirloin steak
1/2 cup low-sodium beef broth
1/4 cup low-sodium soy sauce
2 tablespoons Worcestershire sauce
2 tablespoons tomato paste
1 teaspoon garlic powder
1 teaspoon onion powder
1/2 teaspoon black pepper
1/4 teaspoon cayenne pepper
1 tablespoon olive oil

Directions:
1. Preheat the air fryer to 375°F.
2. In a shallow dish, combine the beef broth, soy sauce, Worcestershire sauce, tomato paste, garlic powder, onion powder, black pepper, and cayenne pepper. Mix until combined.
3. Place the sirloin steak in the shallow dish and coat with the marinade. Let sit for 10 minutes.

4. Place the sirloin steak in the air fryer basket and cook for 8 minutes.
5. Flip the steak and cook for an additional 7 minutes.
6. Remove the steak from the air fryer and let rest for 5 minutes before serving.

Nutrition: Calories: 250 | Total Fat: 8g | Saturated Fat: 2g | Cholesterol: 70mg | Sodium: 600mg | Carbohydrates: 4g | Protein: 34

CHAPTER 3: POULTRY RECIPES

Chicken Nuggets

Prep Time: 10 minutes | **Cook Time:** 15 minutes | **Serve:** 4

Ingredients:
- 2 boneless, skinless chicken breasts, cut into 1-inch cubes
- 1/2 cup whole wheat flour
- 1/4 teaspoon garlic powder
- 1/4 teaspoon onion powder
- 1/4 teaspoon paprika
- 1/4 teaspoon black pepper
- 1/4 teaspoon salt
- 2 tablespoons olive oil

Directions:
1. Preheat air fryer to 400F.
2. In a shallow bowl, mix together the flour, garlic powder, onion powder, paprika, black pepper, and salt.
3. Place the chicken cubes in the flour mixture and toss to coat.
4. Place the chicken cubes in the air fryer basket and drizzle with the olive oil.
5. Cook for 10-15 minutes, or until the chicken is cooked through and golden brown.
6. Serve with your favorite dipping sauce.

Nutrition: Calories: 200 | Fat: 8g | Carbs: 15g | Protein: 15g

Low-Carb Chicken Meatballs

Prep Time: 10 minutes | **Cook Time:** 20 minutes | **Serve:** 4

Ingredients:
-1 lb ground chicken
-1/4 cup grated Parmesan cheese
-1/4 cup almond flour
-1 teaspoon garlic powder

-1 teaspoon onion powder
-1 teaspoon Italian seasoning
-1/2 teaspoon salt
-1/4 teaspoon black pepper
-1 egg
-1 tablespoon olive oil

Directions:
1. Preheat air fryer to 375°F.
2. In a large bowl, mix together ground chicken, Parmesan cheese, almond flour, garlic powder, onion powder, Italian seasoning, salt and pepper.
3. Add egg and mix until combined.
4. Form mixture into 1-inch meatballs.
5. Brush olive oil onto the air fryer basket.
6. Place meatballs in the air fryer basket and cook for 20 minutes, flipping halfway through.

Nutrition: Calories: 199 | Fat: 12g | Carbs: 3g | Protein: 19g

Buffalo Chicken Hot Wings

Prep Time: 10 minutes | **Cook Time:** 20 minutes | **Serve:** 4

Ingredients:
- 2 lbs chicken wings
- 1/4 cup hot sauce
- 2 tablespoons olive oil
- 1 teaspoon garlic powder
- 1 teaspoon onion powder
- 1/2 teaspoon black pepper
- 1/2 teaspoon paprika
- 1/2 teaspoon salt
- 1/2 teaspoon cayenne pepper

Directions:
1. Preheat the air fryer to 400 degrees F.
2. In a large bowl, combine the chicken wings, hot sauce, olive oil, garlic powder, onion powder, black pepper, paprika, salt, and cayenne pepper. Mix until the wings are evenly coated.
3. Place the wings in the air fryer basket and cook for 10 minutes. Flip the wings and cook for an additional 10 minutes.
4. Remove the wings from the air fryer and serve with your favorite dipping sauce.

Nutrition: Calories: 441 | Total Fat: 24g | Saturated Fat: 6g | Cholesterol: 109mg | Sodium: 1608mg | Carbohydrates: 6g | Fiber: 1g | Sugar: 1g | Protein: 43g

Herb Chicken Thighs

Prep Time: 10 minutes | **Cook Time:** 20 minutes | Serves: 4

Ingredients:
- 4 boneless, skinless chicken thighs
- 2 tablespoons olive oil
- 1 teaspoon garlic powder
- 1 teaspoon dried oregano
- 1 teaspoon dried thyme
- 1 teaspoon dried basil
- 1/2 teaspoon sea salt
- 1/4 teaspoon freshly ground black pepper

Directions:
1. Preheat air fryer to 400°F.
2. In a large bowl, combine olive oil, garlic powder, oregano, thyme, basil, salt, and pepper.
3. Add chicken thighs to the bowl and toss to coat.
4. Place chicken thighs in the air fryer basket and cook for 10 minutes.
5. Flip chicken thighs and cook for an additional 10 minutes.

Nutrition: Calories: 200 | Total Fat: 10g | Saturated Fat: 2g | Cholesterol: 75mg | Sodium: 320mg | Carbohydrates: 1g | Fiber: 0g | Protein: 24g

Lemon Pepper Chicken

Prep Time: 10 minutes | **Cook Time:** 20 minutes | **Serve:** 4

Ingredients:
- 4 boneless, skinless chicken breasts
- 2 tablespoons olive oil
- 2 tablespoons lemon juice
- 1 teaspoon garlic powder
- 1 teaspoon onion powder
- 1 teaspoon black pepper
- 1 teaspoon dried oregano
- 1 teaspoon dried basil
- 1 teaspoon paprika
- Salt to taste

Directions:
1. Preheat air fryer to 375°F.
2. In a medium bowl, combine olive oil, lemon juice, garlic powder, onion powder, black pepper, oregano, basil, and paprika.

3. Place chicken breasts in the bowl and coat with the marinade.
4. Place chicken breasts in the air fryer basket and cook for 10 minutes.
5. Flip chicken breasts and cook for an additional 10 minutes.

Nutrition: Calories: 200 | Fat: 9g | Carbs: 2g | Protein: 24g

Mustard Honey Turkey Breast

Prep Time: 10 minutes | **Cook Time:** 25 minutes | Serves: 4

Ingredients:
- 4 boneless, skinless turkey breasts
- 2 tablespoons honey mustard
- 2 tablespoons olive oil
- 1 teaspoon garlic powder
- 1 teaspoon onion powder
- 1 teaspoon paprika
- 1 teaspoon dried oregano
- Salt and pepper to taste

Directions:
1. Preheat air fryer to 400 degrees F.
2. In a small bowl, mix together honey mustard, olive oil, garlic powder, onion powder, paprika, oregano, salt and pepper.
3. Rub the mixture onto the turkey breasts.
4. Place the turkey breasts in the air fryer basket.
5. Cook for 25 minutes or until the internal temperature reaches 165 degrees F.
6. Let the turkey rest for 5 minutes before serving.

Nutrition: Calories: 199 | Fat: 8g | Protein: 28g | Carbs: 4g | Fiber: 0g | Sodium: 586mg

Air Fryer Chicken Cutlets

Prep Time: 10 minutes | **Cook Time:** 15 minutes | **Serve:** 4

Ingredients:
- 4 boneless, skinless chicken cutlets
- 2 tablespoons olive oil
- 1 teaspoon garlic powder
- 1 teaspoon onion powder
- 1 teaspoon paprika
- 1 teaspoon dried oregano
- 1/2 teaspoon salt
- 1/4 teaspoon black pepper

Directions:
1. Preheat air fryer to 400°F.
2. Place chicken cutlets in a shallow dish. Drizzle with olive oil and season with garlic powder, onion powder, paprika, oregano, salt, and pepper. Toss to coat.
3. Place chicken cutlets in the air fryer basket. Cook for 10 minutes, flipping halfway through.
4. Increase heat to 425°F and cook for an additional 5 minutes, or until chicken is cooked through and golden brown.

Nutrition: Calories: 200 | Fat: 10g | Carbohydrates: 1g | Protein: 25g | Sodium: 400mg

Turkey Patties

Prep Time: 10 minutes | **Cook Time:** 10 minutes | **Serve:** 4

Ingredients:
1 lb. ground turkey
1/4 cup breadcrumbs
1/4 cup diced onion
1/4 cup diced bell pepper
1/4 cup diced celery
1 teaspoon garlic powder
1 teaspoon onion powder
1 teaspoon black pepper
1 teaspoon salt
1 teaspoon paprika
1/4 cup low-sodium chicken broth

Directions:
1. In a large bowl, combine the ground turkey, breadcrumbs, onion, bell pepper, celery, garlic powder, onion powder, black pepper, salt, and paprika. Mix until all ingredients are evenly distributed.
2. Form the mixture into 4 patties.
3. Place the patties in the air fryer basket and cook for 10 minutes at 375°F.
4. Once the patties are cooked through, remove from the air fryer and let rest for 5 minutes.
5. Serve with your favorite side dishes.

Nutrition: Calories: 190 | Fat: 8g | Carbohydrates: 8g | Protein: 21g

Rotisserie Chicken Fajitas

Prep Time: 10 minutes | **Cook Time:** 15 minutes | **Serve:** 4

Ingredients:

- 1 rotisserie chicken, shredded
- 2 bell peppers, sliced
- 1 onion, sliced
- 2 tablespoons olive oil
- 1 teaspoon garlic powder
- 1 teaspoon chili powder
- 1 teaspoon cumin
- 1 teaspoon paprika
- 1/2 teaspoon salt
- 1/4 teaspoon black pepper
- 4 whole wheat tortillas

Directions:
1. Preheat the air fryer to 400°F.
2. Place the bell peppers and onion in a large bowl and toss with the olive oil, garlic powder, chili powder, cumin, paprika, salt, and black pepper.
3. Place the bell pepper and onion mixture in the air fryer basket and cook for 10 minutes, stirring halfway through.
4. Add the shredded rotisserie chicken to the air fryer basket and cook for an additional 5 minutes.
5. Serve the fajita mixture in the whole wheat tortillas.

Nutrition: Calories: 437 | Total Fat: 17g | Saturated Fat: 4g | Cholesterol: 81mg | Sodium: 790mg | Carbohydrates: 36g | Fiber: 6g | Sugar: 5g | Protein: 33g

Roasted Vegetable and Chicken Salad

Prep Time: 10 minutes | **Cook Time:** 20 minutes | **Serve:** 4

Ingredients:
- 2 cups of diced chicken breast
- 1 cup of diced bell peppers
- 1 cup of diced onion
- 1 cup of diced zucchini
- 1 cup of diced carrots
- 2 tablespoons of olive oil
- 2 tablespoons of garlic powder
- 2 tablespoons of Italian seasoning
- 1 teaspoon of salt
- 1 teaspoon of black pepper
- 2 tablespoons of lemon juice
- 2 tablespoons of balsamic vinegar
- 2 tablespoons of chopped fresh parsley

Directions:

1. Preheat the air fryer to 400°F.
2. Place the diced chicken, bell peppers, onion, zucchini, and carrots in a large bowl. Add the olive oil, garlic powder, Italian seasoning, salt, and black pepper. Toss to combine.
3. Place the vegetables and chicken in the air fryer basket and cook for 15-20 minutes, stirring halfway through, until the vegetables are tender and the chicken is cooked through.
4. In a small bowl, whisk together the lemon juice, balsamic vinegar, and parsley.
5. Place the cooked vegetables and chicken in a large bowl and pour the dressing over top. Toss to combine.
6. Serve the salad warm or chilled.

Nutrition: Calories: 250 | Total Fat: 10g | Saturated Fat: 2g | Cholesterol: 60mg | Sodium: 500mg | Carbohydrates: 13g | Fiber: 3g | Sugar: 6g | Protein: 25g

Crusted Chicken Drumsticks

Prep Time: 10 minutes | **Cook Time:** 25 minutes | Serves: 4

Ingredients:
- 4 chicken drumsticks
- 2 tablespoons olive oil
- 2 tablespoons almond flour
- 1 teaspoon garlic powder
- 1 teaspoon paprika
- 1 teaspoon dried oregano
- Salt and pepper to taste

Directions:
1. Preheat air fryer to 375°F.
2. In a shallow bowl, combine almond flour, garlic powder, paprika, oregano, salt and pepper. Mix until well combined.
3. Brush chicken drumsticks with olive oil and then coat with the almond flour mixture.
4. Place chicken drumsticks in the air fryer and cook for 25 minutes, flipping halfway through.

Nutrition: Calories: 140 | Total Fat: 8g | Saturated Fat: 1g | Cholesterol: 50mg | Sodium: 140mg | Carbohydrates: 3g | Fiber: 1g | Sugar: 0g | Protein: 14g

Thyme Turkey Breast

Prep Time: 10 minutes | **Cook Time:** 30 minutes | **Serve:** 4

Ingredients:
1 lb. boneless, skinless turkey breast
1 tablespoon olive oil
1 teaspoon garlic powder

1 teaspoon dried thyme
1 teaspoon onion powder
1 teaspoon paprika
1/2 teaspoon black pepper
1/4 teaspoon salt

Directions:
1. Preheat air fryer to 375°F.
2. Rub turkey breast with olive oil, garlic powder, thyme, onion powder, paprika, black pepper, and salt.
3. Place turkey breast in air fryer basket.
4. Cook for 30 minutes, flipping halfway through.
5. Remove from air fryer and let rest for 5 minutes before slicing.

Nutrition: Calories: 140 | Total Fat: 4g | Saturated Fat: 1g | Cholesterol: 70mg | Sodium: 170mg | Carbohydrates: 1g | Fiber: 0g | Protein: 25g

Chicken Wings with Alfredo Sauce

Prep Time: 15 minutes | **Cook Time:** 25 minutes | **Serve:** 4

Ingredients:
2 lbs chicken wings
1/2 cup low-fat Alfredo sauce
1/4 teaspoon garlic powder
1/4 teaspoon onion powder
1/4 teaspoon black pepper
1/4 teaspoon paprika
1/4 teaspoon dried oregano
1/4 teaspoon dried basil

Directions:
1. Preheat air fryer to 375°F.
2. Place chicken wings in a large bowl and season with garlic powder, onion powder, black pepper, paprika, oregano, and basil. Toss to combine.
3. Place chicken wings in the air fryer basket and cook for 20 minutes, flipping halfway through.
4. Remove chicken wings from the air fryer and place in a large bowl. Pour Alfredo sauce over the wings and toss to coat.
5. Place chicken wings back in the air fryer basket and cook for an additional 5 minutes.
6. Serve chicken wings with Alfredo sauce.

Nutrition: Calories: 464 | Fat: 21g | Carbohydrates: 8g | Protein: 56g

Chicken Drumsticks

Prep Time: 10 minutes | **Cook Time:** 25 minutes | **Serve:** 4

Ingredients:
- 8 chicken drumsticks
- 2 tablespoons olive oil
- 1 teaspoon garlic powder
- 1 teaspoon onion powder
- 1 teaspoon paprika
- 1 teaspoon dried oregano
- 1 teaspoon dried basil
- 1/2 teaspoon salt
- 1/4 teaspoon black pepper

Directions:
1. Preheat air fryer to 400°F.
2. In a medium bowl, combine olive oil, garlic powder, onion powder, paprika, oregano, basil, salt, and pepper. Mix until well combined.
3. Add chicken drumsticks to the bowl and toss to coat in the seasoning mixture.
4. Place the chicken drumsticks in the air fryer basket and cook for 20 minutes, flipping halfway through.
5. Increase the temperature to 425°F and cook for an additional 5 minutes.

Nutrition: Calories: 256 | Total Fat: 10.5g | Saturated Fat: 2.3g | Cholesterol: 94mg | Sodium: 467mg | Carbohydrates: 1.2g | Fiber: 0.3g | Protein: 38.2g

Chicken Schnitzel

Prep Time: 10 minutes | **Cook Time:** 10 minutes | **Serve:** 4

Ingredients:
- 4 boneless, skinless chicken breasts
- 1/2 cup almond flour
- 2 tablespoons olive oil
- 1 teaspoon garlic powder
- 1 teaspoon onion powder
- 1 teaspoon paprika
- 1/2 teaspoon salt
- 1/4 teaspoon black pepper
- 2 eggs
- 1/4 cup almond milk
- 1/2 cup bread crumbs

Directions:
1. Cut each chicken breast into two thin cutlets.
2. In a shallow bowl, combine almond flour, garlic powder, onion powder, paprika, salt and pepper.
3. In a separate shallow bowl, whisk together eggs and almond milk.
4. Place bread crumbs in a third shallow bowl.
5. Dip each chicken cutlet in the almond flour mixture, then the egg mixture, and finally the bread crumbs.
6. Place the chicken cutlets in the air fryer and cook at 400°F for 10 minutes, flipping halfway through.

Nutrition: Calories: 217 | Fat: 9g | Carbohydrates: 12g | Protein: 22g | Sodium: 454mg | Fiber: 2g

Chicken Rissoles

Prep Time: 10 minutes | **Cook Time:** 15 minutes | **Serve:** 4

Ingredients:
- 500g chicken mince
- 2 tablespoons of olive oil
- 1 onion, finely diced
- 2 cloves of garlic, minced
- 2 tablespoons of tomato paste
- 1 teaspoon of paprika
- 1 teaspoon of dried oregano
- 1/2 teaspoon of ground cumin
- 1/2 teaspoon of chilli powder
- 1/4 cup of fresh parsley, chopped
- 1/4 cup of grated parmesan cheese
- 1/4 cup of breadcrumbs
- 1/4 cup of almond meal
- 2 eggs
- Salt and pepper to taste

Directions:
1. Preheat the air fryer to 180°C.
2. Heat the olive oil in a large frying pan over medium heat.
3. Add the onion and garlic and cook until softened.
4. Add the chicken mince and cook until browned.
5. Add the tomato paste, paprika, oregano, cumin and chilli powder and cook for a further 2 minutes.
6. Remove from the heat and stir in the parsley, parmesan cheese, breadcrumbs, almond meal, eggs and season with salt and pepper.
7. Divide the mixture into 4 equal portions and shape into rissoles.
8. Place the rissoles into the air fryer basket and cook for 15 minutes, turning halfway through cooking.

9. Serve with a side salad or vegetables.

Nutrition: Calories: 250 | Fat: 13g | Carbohydrates: 11g | Protein: 22g

Japanese Chicken Tenders

Prep Time: 10 minutes | **Cook Time:** 15 minutes | **Serve:** 4

Ingredients:
- 1 lb boneless, skinless chicken tenders
- 2 tablespoons low-sodium soy sauce
- 2 tablespoons rice vinegar
- 1 teaspoon garlic powder
- 1 teaspoon ground ginger
- 1 teaspoon sesame oil
- 2 tablespoons cornstarch
- 2 tablespoons olive oil
- Salt and pepper to taste

Directions:
1. Preheat air fryer to 375°F.
2. In a large bowl, combine chicken tenders, soy sauce, rice vinegar, garlic powder, ground ginger, and sesame oil. Mix until chicken is evenly coated.
3. In a separate bowl, combine cornstarch and olive oil. Mix until combined.
4. Add the cornstarch mixture to the chicken and mix until evenly coated.
5. Place the chicken tenders in the air fryer basket and cook for 15 minutes, flipping halfway through.
6. Remove from air fryer and season with salt and pepper to taste. Serve immediately.

Nutrition: Calories: 240 | Fat: 11g | Carbs: 8g | Protein: 25g

Chicken Satay

Prep Time: 10 minutes | **Cook Time:** 10 minutes | **Serve:** 4

Ingredients:
- 1 lb boneless, skinless chicken breasts, cut into thin strips
- 2 tablespoons low-sodium soy sauce
- 2 tablespoons honey
- 1 tablespoon sesame oil
- 2 cloves garlic, minced
- 1 teaspoon ground ginger
- 1/4 teaspoon ground black pepper
- 2 tablespoons peanut butter

- 4 wooden skewers

Directions:
1. In a medium bowl, combine the soy sauce, honey, sesame oil, garlic, ginger, and black pepper.
2. Add the chicken strips and stir to coat. Cover and refrigerate for at least 30 minutes.
3. Preheat the air fryer to 400°F.
4. Thread the chicken strips onto the skewers.
5. Place the skewers in the air fryer basket and cook for 8-10 minutes, flipping halfway through.
6. In a small bowl, combine the peanut butter and 1 tablespoon of water. Microwave for 30 seconds, stirring halfway through.
7. Drizzle the peanut butter sauce over the cooked chicken skewers and serve.

Nutrition: Calories: 240 | Protein: 24g | Fat: 11g | Carbs: 11g | Fiber: 1g | Sodium: 590mg

Greek Lemon Chicken

Prep Time: 10 minutes | **Cook Time:** 20 minutes | **Serve:** 4

Ingredients:
- 4 boneless, skinless chicken breasts
- 2 tablespoons olive oil
- 2 tablespoons lemon juice
- 1 teaspoon garlic powder
- 1 teaspoon dried oregano
- 1 teaspoon dried basil
- 1/2 teaspoon salt
- 1/4 teaspoon black pepper

Directions:
1. Preheat the air fryer to 400°F.
2. In a medium bowl, combine the olive oil, lemon juice, garlic powder, oregano, basil, salt, and pepper.
3. Place the chicken breasts in the air fryer basket and brush with the olive oil mixture.
4. Cook for 10 minutes, then flip the chicken and brush with the remaining olive oil mixture.
5. Cook for an additional 10 minutes or until the chicken is cooked through.
6. Serve with your favorite sides.

Nutrition: Calories: 178 | Fat: 8g | Carbs: 1g | Protein: 24g

Chicken Casserole

Prep Time: 10 minutes | **Cook Time:** 30 minutes | **Serve:** 4

Ingredients:

- 2 cups cooked, diced chicken
- 1 cup cooked brown rice
- 1 cup low-fat, low-sodium chicken broth
- 1/2 cup diced onion
- 1/2 cup diced bell pepper
- 1/2 cup diced celery
- 1/2 cup diced carrots
- 1/4 cup chopped fresh parsley
- 1 teaspoon garlic powder
- 1/2 teaspoon dried oregano
- 1/2 teaspoon dried thyme
- 1/4 teaspoon black pepper
- 1/4 teaspoon salt
- 2 tablespoons olive oil

Directions:
1. Preheat the air fryer to 350°F.
2. In a large bowl, combine the chicken, rice, broth, onion, bell pepper, celery, carrots, parsley, garlic powder, oregano, thyme, pepper, and salt. Mix until all ingredients are evenly distributed.
3. Grease the air fryer basket with the olive oil.
4. Place the chicken and rice mixture into the air fryer basket and cook for 25-30 minutes, stirring occasionally, until the chicken is cooked through and the rice is tender.

Nutrition: Calories: 250 | Fat: 8g | Carbohydrates: 24g | Protein: 20g | Sodium: 300mg | Fiber: 3g

Ranch Chicken Wings

Prep Time: 10 minutes | **Cook Time:** 20 minutes | **Serve:** 4

Ingredients:
- 2 lbs chicken wings
- 2 tablespoons olive oil
- 1/2 teaspoon garlic powder
- 1/2 teaspoon onion powder
- 1/2 teaspoon paprika
- 1/2 teaspoon dried oregano
- 1/2 teaspoon dried basil
- 1/2 teaspoon black pepper
- 1/4 teaspoon salt
- 1/4 cup low-fat ranch dressing

Directions:
1. Preheat air fryer to 400°F.

2. In a large bowl, combine chicken wings, olive oil, garlic powder, onion powder, paprika, oregano, basil, black pepper, and salt. Toss to coat.
3. Place chicken wings in the air fryer basket and cook for 10 minutes. Flip wings and cook for an additional 10 minutes.
4. Remove wings from the air fryer and place in a large bowl. Pour ranch dressing over the wings and toss to coat.
5. Place wings back in the air fryer basket and cook for an additional 5 minutes.

Nutrition: Calories: 270 | Total Fat: 14g | Saturated Fat: 3g | Cholesterol: 90mg | Sodium: 500mg | Carbohydrates: 2g | Fiber: 0g | Sugar: 0g | Protein: 30g

Chicken Mac and Cheese

Prep Time: 10 minutes | **Cook Time:** 20 minutes | **Serve:** 4

Ingredients:
- 2 cups cooked chicken, diced
- 2 cups cooked macaroni noodles
- 1 cup low-fat cheese, shredded
- 1/2 cup low-fat milk
- 1/4 cup butter
- 1/4 cup all-purpose flour
- 1/4 teaspoon garlic powder
- 1/4 teaspoon onion powder
- 1/4 teaspoon black pepper
- 1/4 teaspoon paprika
- 1/4 teaspoon salt

Directions:
1. Preheat the air fryer to 375 degrees F.
2. In a medium saucepan, melt the butter over medium heat.
3. Add the flour and whisk until combined.
4. Slowly add the milk and whisk until the mixture is smooth.
5. Add the garlic powder, onion powder, black pepper, paprika, and salt. Whisk until combined.
6. Add the cheese and stir until melted.
7. Add the cooked chicken and macaroni noodles to the cheese sauce and stir until combined.
8. Place the mixture in the air fryer basket and cook for 15-20 minutes, stirring occasionally.

Nutrition: Calories: 434 | Fat: 16g | Carbs: 37g | Protein: 28g | Fiber: 2g | Sodium: 545mg

Broccoli Chicken Casserole

Prep Time: 10 minutes | **Cook Time:** 30 minutes | Serves: 4

Ingredients:
- 2 cups cooked, shredded chicken
- 2 cups broccoli florets
- 1/2 cup reduced-fat shredded cheese
- 1/4 cup reduced-fat mayonnaise
- 1/4 cup plain Greek yogurt
- 2 tablespoons freshly squeezed lemon juice
- 1/2 teaspoon garlic powder
- 1/4 teaspoon black pepper
- 1/4 teaspoon salt
- 1/4 cup panko breadcrumbs

Directions:
1. Preheat the air fryer to 350°F.
2. In a large bowl, combine the chicken, broccoli, cheese, mayonnaise, yogurt, lemon juice, garlic powder, black pepper, and salt. Mix until everything is evenly combined.
3. Transfer the mixture to a greased air fryer-safe baking dish. Sprinkle the panko breadcrumbs over the top.
4. Place the baking dish in the air fryer and cook for 25-30 minutes, or until the top is golden brown.

Nutrition: Calories: 323 | Fat: 14g | Protein: 30g | Carbs: 18g | Fiber: 3g | Sodium: 536mg

Chicken Tikka Kebab

Prep Time: 10 minutes | **Cook Time:** 15 minutes | **Serve:** 4

Ingredients:
- 1 lb boneless, skinless chicken breast, cut into 1-inch cubes
- 1/4 cup plain Greek yogurt
- 1 teaspoon garam masala
- 1 teaspoon ground cumin
- 1 teaspoon ground coriander
- 1/2 teaspoon ground turmeric
- 1/2 teaspoon ground ginger
- 1/4 teaspoon cayenne pepper
- 1/2 teaspoon salt
- 1/4 teaspoon black pepper
- 1 tablespoon olive oil

Directions:
1. In a medium bowl, combine the yogurt, garam masala, cumin, coriander, turmeric, ginger, cayenne pepper, salt, and black pepper.
2. Add the chicken cubes and stir to coat. Cover and refrigerate for at least 30 minutes.
3. Preheat the air fryer to 400°F.

4. Place the chicken cubes in the air fryer basket and drizzle with the olive oil.
5. Cook for 12-15 minutes, shaking the basket every 5 minutes, until the chicken is cooked through.
6. Serve with your favorite sides.

Nutrition: Calories: 180 | Total Fat: 6g | Saturated Fat: 1.5g | Cholesterol: 73mg | Sodium: 488mg | Carbohydrates: 2g | Fiber: 0.5g | Sugar: 1g | Protein: 27g

CHAPTER 4: VEGETABLES & SIDE DISHES

Honey Brussels Sprouts

Prep Time: 10 minutes | **Cook Time:** 15 minutes | **Serve:** 4

Ingredients:
- 2 pounds Brussels sprouts, trimmed and halved
- 2 tablespoons olive oil
- 2 tablespoons honey
- 1 teaspoon garlic powder
- 1 teaspoon onion powder
- 1 teaspoon smoked paprika
- Salt and pepper, to taste

Directions:
1. Preheat the air fryer to 375°F.
2. Place the Brussels sprouts in a large bowl and add the olive oil, honey, garlic powder, onion powder, smoked paprika, salt, and pepper. Toss to combine.
3. Place the Brussels sprouts in the air fryer basket and cook for 15 minutes, shaking the basket halfway through.
4. Remove the Brussels sprouts from the air fryer and serve.

Nutrition: Calories: 135 | Total Fat: 5g | Saturated Fat: 1g | Sodium: 70mg | Carbohydrates: 20g | Fiber: 5g | Sugar: 8g | Protein: 5g

Air Fried Tofu

Prep Time: 10 minutes | **Cook Time:** 15 minutes | **Serve:** 4

Ingredients:
- 1 package extra-firm tofu, drained and cut into cubes
- 2 tablespoons olive oil
- 2 tablespoons soy sauce
- 2 tablespoons garlic powder
- 2 tablespoons nutritional yeast

- 1 teaspoon smoked paprika
- Salt and pepper, to taste

Directions:
1. Preheat air fryer to 400°F.
2. Place the tofu cubes in a large bowl and add the olive oil, soy sauce, garlic powder, nutritional yeast, smoked paprika, salt, and pepper. Toss to combine.
3. Place the tofu cubes in the air fryer basket and cook for 15 minutes, shaking the basket halfway through.
4. Remove the tofu from the air fryer and serve.

Nutrition: Calories: 145 | Total Fat: 8g | Saturated Fat: 1g | Cholesterol: 0mg | Sodium: 590mg | Carbohydrates: 5g | Fiber: 1g | Sugar: 0g | Protein: 11g

Roasted Bell Peppers

Prep Time: 10 minutes | **Cook Time:** 15 minutes | **Serve:** 4

Ingredients:
- 4 bell peppers, any color
- 2 tablespoons olive oil
- Salt and pepper, to taste

Directions:
1. Preheat the air fryer to 375°F.
2. Cut the bell peppers into 1-inch slices.
3. Place the bell pepper slices in a bowl and drizzle with olive oil.
4. Season with salt and pepper, to taste.
5. Place the bell pepper slices in the air fryer basket and cook for 15 minutes.

Nutrition: Calories: 70 | Fat: 5g | Carbohydrates: 5g | Protein: 1g | Sodium: 10mg

Air Fried Pickles

Prep Time: 10 minutes | **Cook Time:** 10 minutes | **Serve:** 4

Ingredients:
- 1/2 cup all-purpose flour
- 1/2 teaspoon garlic powder
- 1/2 teaspoon onion powder
- 1/2 teaspoon paprika
- 1/4 teaspoon black pepper
- 1/4 teaspoon sea salt
- 1/4 teaspoon dried oregano

- 1/4 teaspoon dried thyme
- 1/4 teaspoon dried basil
- 1/4 teaspoon cayenne pepper
- 1/4 cup low-fat buttermilk
- 1/4 cup panko breadcrumbs
- 1/4 cup grated Parmesan cheese
- 2 cups sliced pickles
- 2 tablespoons olive oil

Directions:
1. Preheat air fryer to 350°F.
2. In a shallow bowl, combine the flour, garlic powder, onion powder, paprika, black pepper, sea salt, oregano, thyme, basil and cayenne pepper.
3. In a separate shallow bowl, combine the buttermilk and panko breadcrumbs.
4. Dip the pickles in the flour mixture, then the buttermilk mixture, and then the Parmesan cheese.
5. Place the pickles in the air fryer basket and drizzle with olive oil.
6. Cook for 10 minutes, shaking the basket halfway through.

Nutrition: Calories: 140 | Fat: 7g | Carbohydrates: 14g | Protein: 5g | Sodium: 360mg | Fiber: 1g | Sugar: 1g

Zucchini Pizza

Prep Time: 10 minutes | **Cook Time:** 15 minutes | **Serve:** 4

Ingredients:
- 2 medium zucchini, sliced into 1/4 inch thick rounds
- 1/2 cup marinara sauce
- 1/2 cup shredded mozzarella cheese
- 1/4 cup grated Parmesan cheese
- 1/4 cup chopped fresh basil
- 1/4 teaspoon garlic powder
- 1/4 teaspoon dried oregano
- Salt and pepper to taste

Directions:
1. Preheat air fryer to 375°F.
2. Place zucchini slices in a single layer in the air fryer basket.
3. Cook for 5 minutes, flipping halfway through.
4. Remove zucchini from the air fryer and place on a plate.
5. Top each zucchini slice with marinara sauce, mozzarella cheese, Parmesan cheese, basil, garlic powder, oregano, salt, and pepper.
6. Place the zucchini slices back in the air fryer and cook for an additional 10 minutes, flipping halfway through.

Nutrition: Calories: 134 | Protein: 8g | Fat: 7g | Carbs: 10g | Fiber: 2g | Sugar: 4g | Sodium: 441mg

Garlic-Roasted Bell Peppers

Prep Time: 10 minutes | **Cook Time:** 15 minutes | Serves: 4

Ingredients:
- 4 bell peppers, cut into 1-inch pieces
- 2 tablespoons olive oil
- 2 cloves garlic, minced
- 1 teaspoon dried oregano
- 1 teaspoon dried basil
- Salt and pepper to taste

Directions:
1. Preheat the air fryer to 400 degrees F.
2. Place the bell peppers in the air fryer basket and cook for 8 minutes.
3. In a small bowl, mix together the olive oil, garlic, oregano, basil, salt, and pepper.
4. After 8 minutes, remove the bell peppers from the air fryer and toss with the olive oil mixture.
5. Place the bell peppers back in the air fryer basket and cook for an additional 7 minutes.

Nutrition: Calories: 80 | Total Fat: 6g | Saturated Fat: 1g | Cholesterol: 0mg | Sodium: 60mg | Total Carbohydrate: 6g | Dietary Fiber: 2g | Sugars: 3g | Protein: 1g

Sweet Corn Fritters with Avocado

Prep Time: 10 minutes | **Cook Time:** 15 minutes | **Serve:** 4

Ingredients:
- 2 cups of frozen sweet corn
- 2 tablespoons of all-purpose flour
- 2 tablespoons of cornstarch
- 1/4 teaspoon of baking powder
- 1/4 teaspoon of salt
- 2 tablespoons of olive oil
- 2 tablespoons of chopped fresh cilantro
- 1/4 cup of diced red onion
- 1/4 cup of diced red bell pepper
- 1/4 cup of diced jalapeno pepper
- 1/4 cup of diced avocado
- 2 tablespoons of freshly squeezed lime juice

Directions:

1. Preheat the air fryer to 350 degrees F.
2. In a medium bowl, combine the sweet corn, flour, cornstarch, baking powder, and salt. Stir until the ingredients are well combined.
3. Add the olive oil, cilantro, red onion, red bell pepper, jalapeno pepper, and avocado. Stir until the ingredients are well combined.
4. Using a spoon, scoop the mixture into the air fryer basket.
5. Cook for 15 minutes, flipping the fritters halfway through.
6. Remove from the air fryer and serve with freshly squeezed lime juice.

Nutrition: Calories: 127 | Fat: 7g | Carbohydrates: 14g | Protein: 2g | Fiber: 2g | Sodium: 186mg

Fried Green Beans with Pecorino Romano

Prep Time: 10 minutes | **Cook Time:** 15 minutes | **Serve:** 4

Ingredients:
- 1 lb fresh green beans, trimmed
- 2 tablespoons olive oil
- 1/4 cup Pecorino Romano cheese, grated
- Salt and pepper, to taste

Directions:
1. Preheat air fryer to 400°F.
2. Place green beans in a large bowl and drizzle with olive oil. Toss to coat.
3. Place green beans in the air fryer basket and cook for 10 minutes, shaking the basket every 5 minutes.
4. Remove from the air fryer and transfer to a serving dish. Sprinkle with Pecorino Romano cheese and season with salt and pepper, to taste.

Nutrition: Calories: 153 kcal | Carbohydrates: 8 g | Protein: 5 g | Fat: 11 g | Saturated Fat: 3 g | Cholesterol: 8 mg | Sodium: 167 mg | Potassium: 233 mg | Fiber: 3 g | Sugar: 3 g | Vitamin A: 745 IU | Vitamin C: 15.3 mg | Calcium: 132 mg | Iron: 1.3 mg

Corn on the Cob with Herb Butter

Prep Time: 5 minutes | **Cook Time:** 15 minutes | **Serve:** 4

Ingredients:
4 ears of corn, husks and silks removed
4 tablespoons of butter, softened
1 teaspoon of fresh chopped parsley
1 teaspoon of fresh chopped chives
1 teaspoon of fresh chopped thyme
1/2 teaspoon of garlic powder

Salt and pepper to taste

Directions:
1. Preheat the air fryer to 400°F.
2. Place the corn in the air fryer basket and cook for 15 minutes, flipping the corn halfway through the cooking time.
3. Meanwhile, in a small bowl, mix together the butter, parsley, chives, thyme, garlic powder, salt and pepper.
4. When the corn is finished cooking, remove it from the air fryer and spread the herb butter over the top.

Nutrition: Calories: 100 | Total Fat: 7g | Saturated Fat: 4g | Cholesterol: 20mg | Sodium: 140mg | Carbohydrates: 8g | Dietary Fiber: 2g | Sugars: 2g | Protein: 2g

Family Vegetable Gratin

Prep Time: 10 minutes | **Cook Time:** 25 minutes | **Serve:** 4

Ingredients:
- 2 cups of cauliflower florets
- 2 cups of broccoli florets
- 1 cup of diced carrots
- 1 cup of diced celery
- 1/2 cup of diced onions
- 1/2 cup of grated Parmesan cheese
- 2 tablespoons of olive oil
- 1/2 teaspoon of garlic powder
- 1/2 teaspoon of dried oregano
- Salt and pepper to taste

Directions:
1. Preheat the air fryer to 375°F.
2. In a large bowl, combine the cauliflower, broccoli, carrots, celery, onions, Parmesan cheese, olive oil, garlic powder, oregano, salt, and pepper. Toss to combine.
3. Place the vegetable mixture in the air fryer basket and cook for 15 minutes.
4. Remove the basket from the air fryer and stir the vegetables. Return the basket to the air fryer and cook for an additional 10 minutes.
5. Serve the vegetable gratin warm.

Nutrition: Calories: 150 | Total Fat: 8g | Saturated Fat: 2g | Cholesterol: 5mg | Sodium: 200mg | Carbohydrates: 13g | Fiber: 4g | Sugar: 4g | Protein: 7g

Crispy Tofu In Asian Sauce

Prep Time: 10 minutes | **Cook Time:** 15 minutes | **Serve:** 4

Ingredients:
- 1 block of extra-firm tofu, drained and cut into cubes
- 1 tablespoon of olive oil
- 2 tablespoons of low-sodium soy sauce
- 1 tablespoon of honey
- 2 tablespoons of rice vinegar
- 2 cloves of garlic, minced
- 1 teaspoon of freshly grated ginger
- 1 teaspoon of sesame oil
- 2 tablespoons of cornstarch
- 1/4 teaspoon of red pepper flakes
- 2 tablespoons of chopped green onions
- Sesame seeds for garnish

Directions:
1. Preheat the air fryer to 400°F.
2. Place the tofu cubes in a large bowl and add the olive oil. Toss to coat.
3. In a small bowl, whisk together the soy sauce, honey, rice vinegar, garlic, ginger, sesame oil, cornstarch, and red pepper flakes.
4. Pour the sauce over the tofu and toss to coat.
5. Place the tofu cubes in the air fryer basket in a single layer.
6. Cook for 15 minutes, shaking the basket halfway through, until the tofu is golden and crispy.
7. Remove the tofu from the air fryer and sprinkle with green onions and sesame seeds.

Nutrition: Calories: 140 | Total Fat: 7g | Saturated Fat: 1g | Cholesterol: 0mg | Sodium: 590mg | Carbohydrates: 11g | Fiber: 1g | Sugar: 5g | Protein: 8g

Crispy Blooming Onion

Prep Time: 10 minutes | **Cook Time:** 10 minutes | **Serve:** 4

Ingredients:
1 large onion
1/4 cup almond flour
1/4 cup arrowroot powder
1/4 teaspoon garlic powder
1/4 teaspoon onion powder
1/4 teaspoon paprika

1/4 teaspoon salt
1/4 teaspoon pepper
1/4 cup unsweetened almond milk
1 tablespoon olive oil

Directions:
1. Preheat air fryer to 400°F.
2. Cut the onion into 1/2-inch thick slices, then separate the slices into petals.
3. In a shallow bowl, mix together the almond flour, arrowroot powder, garlic powder, onion powder, paprika, salt, and pepper.
4. In a separate shallow bowl, mix together the almond milk and olive oil.
5. Dip each onion petal into the almond milk mixture, then into the flour mixture, coating both sides.
6. Place the coated onion petals in the air fryer basket and cook for 10 minutes, flipping halfway through.

Nutrition: Calories: 90 | Total Fat: 5g | Saturated Fat: 1g | Cholesterol: 0mg | Sodium: 170mg | Carbohydrates: 10g | Fiber: 2g | Sugar: 2g | Protein: 3g

Fried Okra

Prep Time: 10 minutes | **Cook Time:** 10 minutes | **Serve:** 4

Ingredients:
-1 lb fresh okra, sliced into 1/4 inch thick pieces
-1/2 cup cornmeal
-1/4 cup grated Parmesan cheese
-1 teaspoon garlic powder
-1/2 teaspoon salt
-1/4 teaspoon black pepper
-1/4 cup olive oil

Directions:
1. Preheat air fryer to 400 degrees F.
2. In a medium bowl, combine the cornmeal, Parmesan cheese, garlic powder, salt and pepper.
3. Place the okra slices in the bowl and toss to coat.
4. Drizzle the olive oil over the okra and toss to coat.
5. Place the okra in the air fryer basket and cook for 8-10 minutes, shaking the basket every few minutes.

Nutrition: Calories: 140 | Fat: 8g | Carbohydrates: 12g | Protein: 4g | Sodium: 260mg | Fiber: 2g

Vegetarian Fajitas

Prep Time: 10 minutes | **Cook Time:** 15 minutes | **Serve:** 4

Ingredients:
- 2 bell peppers, sliced
- 1 onion, sliced
- 1 tablespoon olive oil
- 2 cloves garlic, minced
- 1 teaspoon chili powder
- 1 teaspoon cumin
- 1 teaspoon paprika
- 1/2 teaspoon oregano
- 1/4 teaspoon salt
- 1/4 teaspoon black pepper
- 2 cups cooked black beans
- 4 whole wheat tortillas
- 1/2 cup shredded cheese
- 1/4 cup salsa
- 1/4 cup plain Greek yogurt

Directions:
1. Preheat air fryer to 400 degrees F.
2. Place bell peppers and onion in a large bowl and toss with olive oil.
3. Add garlic, chili powder, cumin, paprika, oregano, salt, and pepper and toss to combine.
4. Place vegetables in the air fryer basket and cook for 10 minutes, stirring halfway through.
5. Meanwhile, warm black beans in a small saucepan over medium heat.
6. Warm tortillas in the air fryer for 1-2 minutes.
7. To assemble the fajitas, place a few spoonfuls of black beans on each tortilla, followed by the cooked vegetables, cheese, salsa, and Greek yogurt.
8. Roll up the tortillas and serve.

Nutrition: Calories: 320 | Fat: 10g | Carbs: 42g | Protein: 13g | Fiber: 8g | Sodium: 488mg

General Tso's Cauliflower

Prep Time: 10 minutes | **Cook Time:** 15 minutes | **Serve:** 4

Ingredients:
- 1 head of cauliflower, cut into florets
- 2 tablespoons of olive oil
- 1/4 cup of low-sodium soy sauce
- 2 tablespoons of rice vinegar
- 2 tablespoons of honey

- 1 teaspoon of garlic powder
- 1 teaspoon of ground ginger
- 1/4 teaspoon of red pepper flakes
- 1/4 cup of cornstarch
- 2 tablespoons of sesame seeds

Directions:
1. Preheat the air fryer to 400°F.
2. In a large bowl, combine the cauliflower florets and olive oil. Toss to coat.
3. In a separate bowl, whisk together the soy sauce, rice vinegar, honey, garlic powder, ground ginger, and red pepper flakes.
4. Place the cauliflower florets in the air fryer basket. Cook for 10 minutes, shaking the basket halfway through.
5. In a shallow dish, combine the cornstarch and sesame seeds. Toss the cooked cauliflower in the cornstarch mixture to coat.
6. Place the coated cauliflower back in the air fryer basket and cook for an additional 5 minutes.
7. Remove the cauliflower from the air fryer and toss with the soy sauce mixture. Serve warm.

Nutrition: Calories: 140 | Fat: 5g | Sodium: 590mg | Carbohydrates: 20g | Fiber: 4g | Protein: 4g

Fried Peppers with Sriracha Mayo

Prep Time: 10 minutes | **Cook Time:** 15 minutes | Serves: 4

Ingredients:
- 2 bell peppers, sliced into strips
- 2 tablespoons olive oil
- 1/2 teaspoon garlic powder
- 1/2 teaspoon salt
- 1/4 teaspoon black pepper
- 1/4 cup mayonnaise
- 1 tablespoon Sriracha sauce

Directions:
1. Preheat air fryer to 400°F.
2. Place bell pepper strips in a large bowl. Drizzle with olive oil and season with garlic powder, salt, and pepper. Toss to combine.
3. Place bell pepper strips in the air fryer basket in a single layer. Cook for 15 minutes, shaking the basket halfway through.
4. In a small bowl, combine mayonnaise and Sriracha sauce.
5. Serve bell pepper strips with Sriracha mayo.

Nutrition: Calories: 125 | Total Fat: 11g | Saturated Fat: 2g | Cholesterol: 5mg | Sodium: 310mg | Carbohydrates: 6g | Fiber: 1g | Sugar: 3g | Protein: 1g

Classic Fried Pickles

Prep Time: 10 minutes | **Cook Time:** 15 minutes | **Serve:** 4-6

Ingredients:
- 1/2 cup almond flour
- 1/2 teaspoon garlic powder
- 1/2 teaspoon onion powder
- 1/2 teaspoon smoked paprika
- 1/4 teaspoon sea salt
- 1/4 teaspoon black pepper
- 1/4 teaspoon cayenne pepper
- 1/4 cup water
- 1 large egg
- 1 pound pickle slices
- 2 tablespoons olive oil

Directions:
1. Preheat air fryer to 380 degrees F.
2. In a shallow bowl, mix together almond flour, garlic powder, onion powder, smoked paprika, sea salt, black pepper, and cayenne pepper.
3. In a separate shallow bowl, whisk together water and egg.
4. Dip pickle slices into egg mixture, then coat with almond flour mixture.
5. Place pickle slices in air fryer basket and spray with olive oil.
6. Cook for 15 minutes, flipping halfway through.

Nutrition: Calories: 128 | Total Fat: 8g | Saturated Fat: 1g | Cholesterol: 37mg | Sodium: 886mg | Carbohydrates: 8g | Fiber: 2g | Sugar: 1g | Protein: 5g

Tofu Tikka

Prep Time: 10 minutes | **Cook Time:** 15 minutes | **Serve:** 4

Ingredients:
- 1 block of extra-firm tofu, drained and cut into cubes
- 1/4 cup plain Greek yogurt
- 2 tablespoons olive oil
- 2 tablespoons lemon juice
- 1 teaspoon garam masala
- 1 teaspoon ground cumin
- 1 teaspoon ground coriander
- 1/2 teaspoon ground turmeric
- 1/2 teaspoon ground ginger
- 1/2 teaspoon garlic powder

- 1/2 teaspoon onion powder
- Salt and pepper, to taste

Directions:
1. Preheat the air fryer to 375°F.
2. In a large bowl, combine the yogurt, olive oil, lemon juice, garam masala, cumin, coriander, turmeric, ginger, garlic powder, onion powder, salt, and pepper. Mix until combined.
3. Add the tofu cubes to the bowl and gently toss to coat.
4. Place the tofu cubes in the air fryer basket and cook for 15 minutes, flipping halfway through.
5. Serve the tofu tikka with your favorite sides.

Nutrition: Calories: 139 | Total Fat: 9g | Saturated Fat: 1g | Cholesterol: 0mg | Sodium: 39mg | Carbohydrates: 6g | Fiber: 1g | Sugar: 2g | Protein: 9g

Spicy Glazed Carrots

Prep Time: 10 minutes | **Cook Time:** 20 minutes | **Serve:** 4

Ingredients:
2 pounds carrots, peeled and cut into 1/2 inch slices
2 tablespoons olive oil
1 teaspoon garlic powder
1 teaspoon chili powder
1 teaspoon smoked paprika
1/2 teaspoon ground cumin
1/4 teaspoon ground cinnamon
1/4 teaspoon ground nutmeg
1/4 teaspoon ground ginger
2 tablespoons honey
2 tablespoons apple cider vinegar
Salt and pepper to taste

Directions:
1. Preheat the air fryer to 400°F.
2. Place the carrots in a large bowl and add the olive oil, garlic powder, chili powder, smoked paprika, cumin, cinnamon, nutmeg, and ginger. Toss to combine.
3. Place the carrots in the air fryer basket and cook for 15 minutes, shaking the basket halfway through.
4. In a small bowl, whisk together the honey and apple cider vinegar.
5. After the carrots have cooked for 15 minutes, remove the basket from the air fryer and pour the honey-vinegar mixture over the carrots. Toss to combine.
6. Return the basket to the air fryer and cook for an additional 5 minutes.
7. Remove the basket from the air fryer and season with salt and pepper to taste. Serve warm.

Nutrition: Calories: 128 | Total Fat: 5g | Saturated Fat: 1g | Cholesterol: 0mg | Sodium: 21mg | Carbohydrates: 20g | Fiber: 4g | Sugar: 12g | Protein: 2g

Rainbow Vegetable Fritters

Prep Time: 10 minutes | **Cook Time:** 15 minutes | **Serve:** 4

Ingredients:
- 1/2 cup grated carrots
- 1/2 cup grated zucchini
- 1/2 cup grated red bell pepper
- 1/2 cup grated yellow bell pepper
- 1/2 cup grated sweet potato
- 1/4 cup chopped fresh parsley
- 2 tablespoons chopped fresh chives
- 2 tablespoons chopped fresh dill
- 1/2 cup all-purpose flour
- 1/2 teaspoon baking powder
- 1/4 teaspoon salt
- 1/4 teaspoon ground black pepper
- 2 large eggs, lightly beaten
- 2 tablespoons olive oil

Directions:
1. Preheat air fryer to 375°F.
2. In a large bowl, combine the carrots, zucchini, bell peppers, sweet potato, parsley, chives, and dill.
3. In a separate bowl, whisk together the flour, baking powder, salt, and pepper.
4. Add the eggs and olive oil to the dry ingredients and mix until combined.
5. Add the wet ingredients to the vegetables and mix until combined.
6. Form the mixture into small patties and place in the air fryer basket.
7. Cook for 15 minutes, flipping halfway through.

Nutrition: Calories: 120 | Fat: 6g | Carbohydrates: 12g | Protein: 4g | Fiber: 2g

Balsamic Root Vegetables

Prep Time: 10 minutes | **Cook Time:** 15 minutes | **Serve:** 4

Ingredients:
- 2 large sweet potatoes, peeled and cut into cubes
- 2 large carrots, peeled and cut into cubes
- 2 large parsnips, peeled and cut into cubes
- 2 tablespoons olive oil
- 2 tablespoons balsamic vinegar

- 1 teaspoon garlic powder
- 1 teaspoon dried oregano
- Salt and pepper, to taste

Directions:
1. Preheat air fryer to 400°F.
2. Place the sweet potatoes, carrots, and parsnips into a large bowl.
3. Drizzle with olive oil and balsamic vinegar, then sprinkle with garlic powder, oregano, salt, and pepper. Toss to coat.
4. Place the vegetables into the air fryer basket and cook for 15 minutes, shaking the basket halfway through.

Nutrition: Calories: 120 | Total Fat: 5g | Saturated Fat: 1g | Sodium: 150mg | Carbohydrates: 18g | Fiber: 4g | Sugar: 5g | Protein: 2g

CHAPTER 5: FISH AND SEAFOOD RECIPES

Tomato Basil Scallops

Prep Time: 10 minutes | **Cook Time:** 15 minutes | **Serve:** 4

Ingredients:
- 1 lb large sea scallops
- 2 tablespoons olive oil
- 2 cloves garlic, minced
- 2 tablespoons fresh basil, chopped
- 1/2 teaspoon salt
- 1/4 teaspoon black pepper
- 1/2 cup cherry tomatoes, halved
- 2 tablespoons Parmesan cheese, grated

Directions:
1. Preheat air fryer to 400°F.
2. In a medium bowl, combine scallops, olive oil, garlic, basil, salt and pepper. Mix until scallops are evenly coated.
3. Place scallops in the air fryer basket and cook for 8 minutes.
4. Add cherry tomatoes to the air fryer basket and cook for an additional 5 minutes.
5. Remove from air fryer and sprinkle with Parmesan cheese. Serve immediately.

Nutrition: Calories: 170 | Total Fat: 8g | Saturated Fat: 2g | Cholesterol: 40mg | Sodium: 330mg | Carbohydrates: 4g | Fiber: 1g | Sugar: 2g | Protein: 19g

Shrimp Scampi

Prep Time: 10 minutes | **Cook Time:** 10 minutes | **Serve:** 4

Ingredients:
- 1 pound of shrimp, peeled and deveined
- 2 tablespoons of olive oil
- 2 tablespoons of lemon juice
- 2 cloves of garlic, minced
- 1 teaspoon of dried oregano
- 1 teaspoon of dried basil
- 1 teaspoon of salt
- 1/2 teaspoon of black pepper
- 2 tablespoons of fresh parsley, chopped

Directions:
1. Preheat the air fryer to 375°F.
2. In a medium bowl, combine the shrimp, olive oil, lemon juice, garlic, oregano, basil, salt, and pepper. Mix until the shrimp is evenly coated.
3. Place the shrimp in the air fryer basket and cook for 8-10 minutes, or until the shrimp is cooked through.
4. Remove the shrimp from the air fryer and transfer to a serving plate.
5. Sprinkle with fresh parsley and serve.

Nutrition: Calories: 200 | Total Fat: 8g | Saturated Fat: 1g | Cholesterol: 172mg | Sodium: 740mg | Carbohydrates: 3g | Fiber: 1g | Protein: 24g

Cilantro Lime Shrimps

Prep Time: 10 minutes | **Cook Time:** 10 minutes | **Serve:** 4

Ingredients:
- 1 lb. raw shrimp, peeled and deveined
- 2 tablespoons olive oil
- 2 tablespoons lime juice
- 1 teaspoon garlic powder
- 1 teaspoon chili powder
- 1 teaspoon ground cumin
- 1/4 teaspoon salt
- 1/4 teaspoon black pepper
- 2 tablespoons chopped fresh cilantro

Directions:
1. Preheat air fryer to 400°F.

2. In a medium bowl, combine shrimp, olive oil, lime juice, garlic powder, chili powder, cumin, salt, and pepper. Toss to coat.
3. Place shrimp in air fryer basket and cook for 8 minutes, shaking basket halfway through.
4. Remove from air fryer and transfer to a serving dish. Sprinkle with cilantro and serve.

Nutrition: Calories: 155 | Total Fat: 7g | Saturated Fat: 1g | Cholesterol: 172mg | Sodium: 437mg | Carbohydrates: 2g | Fiber: 0g | Sugar: 0g | Protein: 19g

Breaded Sea Scallops

Prep Time: 10 minutes | **Cook Time:** 10 minutes | **Serve:** 4

Ingredients:
- 1 lb sea scallops
- 1/2 cup almond flour
- 1/2 teaspoon garlic powder
- 1/2 teaspoon paprika
- 1/2 teaspoon sea salt
- 1/4 teaspoon black pepper
- 1/4 teaspoon onion powder
- 2 tablespoons olive oil

Directions:
1. Preheat the air fryer to 400°F.
2. In a shallow bowl, mix together the almond flour, garlic powder, paprika, sea salt, black pepper, and onion powder.
3. Rinse the scallops and pat dry with a paper towel.
4. Place the scallops in the bowl with the almond flour mixture and coat them evenly.
5. Drizzle the olive oil over the scallops and mix until evenly coated.
6. Place the scallops in the air fryer basket and cook for 10 minutes.

Nutrition: Calories: 200 | Carbohydrates: 5g | Protein: 22g | Fat: 10g | Sodium: 400mg

Crumbed Fish

Prep Time: 10 minutes | **Cook Time:** 15 minutes | **Serve:** 2

Ingredients:
2 pieces of white fish fillets
3 tablespoons of almond flour
2 tablespoons of Parmesan cheese
1 teaspoon of garlic powder
1 teaspoon of paprika
1 teaspoon of dried oregano

1 teaspoon of dried basil
1/2 teaspoon of salt
1/4 teaspoon of black pepper
1 egg, beaten
1 tablespoon of olive oil

Directions:
1. Preheat the air fryer to 375°F.
2. In a shallow bowl, mix together the almond flour, Parmesan cheese, garlic powder, paprika, oregano, basil, salt, and pepper.
3. In another shallow bowl, beat the egg.
4. Dip each fish fillet in the egg, then in the flour mixture, coating both sides.
5. Place the fish in the air fryer basket and lightly spray with olive oil.
6. Cook for 15 minutes, flipping the fish halfway through.

Nutrition: Calories: 270 | Total Fat: 13g | Saturated Fat: 3g | Cholesterol: 115mg | Sodium: 690mg | Carbohydrates: 8g | Fiber: 3g | Sugar: 1g | Protein: 29g

Salmon Cakes with Sriracha Mayo

Prep Time: 10 minutes | **Cook Time:** 10 minutes | Serves: 4

Ingredients:
-1 lb salmon, cooked and flaked
-1/4 cup green onions, chopped
-1/4 cup red bell pepper, diced
-1/4 cup bread crumbs
-1 egg, beaten
-1 teaspoon garlic powder
-1 teaspoon onion powder
-1/4 teaspoon salt
-1/4 teaspoon black pepper
-1/4 cup olive oil

For the Sriracha Mayo:
-1/2 cup mayonnaise
-2 tablespoons sriracha sauce

Directions:
1. In a large bowl, combine the salmon, green onions, red bell pepper, bread crumbs, egg, garlic powder, onion powder, salt, and black pepper. Mix until everything is evenly combined.
2. Form the mixture into 8 patties.
3. Heat the olive oil in the air fryer to 350°F.
4. Place the patties in the air fryer and cook for 5 minutes. Flip the patties and cook for an additional 5 minutes.

5. To make the Sriracha Mayo, combine the mayonnaise and sriracha in a small bowl and mix until evenly combined.
6. Serve the salmon cakes with the Sriracha Mayo.

Nutrition: Calories: 478 | Fat: 33g | Protein: 28g | Carbs: 15g | Fiber: 1g | Sugar: 2g | Sodium: 564mg

Lemon Pepper Shrimp

Prep Time: 10 minutes | **Cook Time:** 10 minutes | **Serve:** 4

Ingredients:
1 lb. large shrimp, peeled and deveined
2 tbsp. olive oil
2 tsp. lemon pepper seasoning
1 lemon, cut into wedges

Directions:
1. Preheat air fryer to 400°F.
2. Place shrimp in a bowl and drizzle with olive oil. Toss to coat.
3. Sprinkle lemon pepper seasoning over shrimp and toss to coat.
4. Place shrimp in air fryer basket in a single layer.
5. Cook for 8-10 minutes, or until shrimp are cooked through and lightly golden.
6. Serve with lemon wedges.

Nutrition: Calories: 160 | Total Fat: 8g | Saturated Fat: 1g | Cholesterol: 172mg | Sodium: 590mg | Carbohydrates: 3g | Fiber: 0g | Sugar: 0g | Protein: 19g

Lobster Tails with Garlic-Lemon Butter

Prep Time: 10 minutes | **Cook Time:** 10 minutes | **Serve:** 4

Ingredients:
4 lobster tails
4 tablespoons butter, melted
2 cloves garlic, minced
2 tablespoons lemon juice
1 tablespoon parsley, chopped
Salt and pepper, to taste

Directions:
1. Preheat the air fryer to 400 degrees F.
2. Cut the lobster tails in half lengthwise and remove the vein.
3. In a small bowl, mix together the melted butter, garlic, lemon juice, parsley, salt and pepper.

4. Place the lobster tails in the air fryer basket and brush with the garlic-lemon butter.
5. Cook for 10 minutes, or until the lobster is cooked through and the shells are golden brown.
6. Serve with additional garlic-lemon butter and enjoy!

Nutrition: Calories: 206 | Fat: 13g | Carbohydrates: 1g | Protein: 22g

Coconut Shrimp

Prep Time: 10 minutes | **Cook Time:** 10 minutes | **Serve:** 4

Ingredients:
-1 lb. raw shrimp, peeled and deveined
-1/2 cup unsweetened shredded coconut
-1/4 cup almond flour
-1/4 teaspoon garlic powder
-1/4 teaspoon salt
-1/4 teaspoon black pepper
-1 large egg, beaten
-2 tablespoons olive oil

Directions:
1. Preheat the air fryer to 375°F.
2. In a shallow bowl, combine the coconut, almond flour, garlic powder, salt, and pepper.
3. In a separate shallow bowl, beat the egg.
4. Dip the shrimp into the egg, then into the coconut mixture, making sure to coat evenly.
5. Place the shrimp in the air fryer basket and drizzle with the olive oil.
6. Cook for 10 minutes, flipping the shrimp halfway through.

Nutrition: Calories: 225 | Fat: 13g | Carbohydrates: 10g | Protein: 16g | Fiber: 3g | Sodium: 462mg

Lemon Chili Salmon

Prep Time: 10 minutes | **Cook Time:** 15 minutes | **Serve:** 4

Ingredients:
4 salmon fillets
2 tablespoons olive oil
2 tablespoons lemon juice
1 teaspoon chili powder
1 teaspoon garlic powder
1 teaspoon onion powder
1 teaspoon dried oregano
1 teaspoon dried thyme
1 teaspoon paprika

1 teaspoon sea salt
1 teaspoon black pepper

Directions:
1. Preheat the air fryer to 375°F.
2. In a medium bowl, combine the olive oil, lemon juice, chili powder, garlic powder, onion powder, oregano, thyme, paprika, sea salt, and black pepper.
3. Place the salmon fillets in the air fryer basket and brush the mixture over the top of the salmon.
4. Cook for 15 minutes, or until the salmon is cooked through.
5. Serve the salmon with your favorite sides.

Nutrition: Calories: 250 | Protein: 24g | Fat: 14g | Carbohydrates: 2g | Fiber: 0g | Sodium: 590mg

Tuna Burgers

Prep Time: 10 minutes | **Cook Time:** 10 minutes | **Serve:** 4

Ingredients:
- 2 cans of tuna, drained
- 2 tablespoons of olive oil
- 1/2 cup of diced onion
- 1/2 cup of diced celery
- 1/2 cup of diced red pepper
- 2 tablespoons of lemon juice
- 1/2 teaspoon of garlic powder
- 1/2 teaspoon of dried oregano
- 1/4 teaspoon of ground black pepper
- 1/4 teaspoon of sea salt
- 1/2 cup of gluten-free breadcrumbs

Directions:
1. Preheat the air fryer to 375°F.
2. In a large bowl, combine the tuna, olive oil, onion, celery, red pepper, lemon juice, garlic powder, oregano, black pepper, and sea salt. Mix until everything is well combined.
3. Form the mixture into 4 patties.
4. Place the patties in the air fryer basket and cook for 8 minutes.
5. Remove the patties from the air fryer and coat each patty with the breadcrumbs.
6. Place the patties back in the air fryer and cook for an additional 2 minutes.

Nutrition: Calories: 200 | Total Fat: 8g | Saturated Fat: 1g | Cholesterol: 25mg | Sodium: 230mg | Carbohydrates: 12g | Fiber: 2g | Sugar: 2g | Protein: 17g

Breaded Cod

Prep Time: 10 minutes | **Cook Time:** 15 minutes | **Serve:** 4

Ingredients:
4 cod fillets
1/2 cup panko bread crumbs
1/4 cup grated Parmesan cheese
1 teaspoon garlic powder
1 teaspoon Italian seasoning
1/4 teaspoon salt
1/4 teaspoon black pepper
1 egg, lightly beaten
2 tablespoons olive oil

Directions:
1. Preheat air fryer to 400°F.
2. In a shallow bowl, combine the panko, Parmesan, garlic powder, Italian seasoning, salt, and pepper.
3. Place the egg in a separate shallow bowl.
4. Dip each cod fillet into the egg, then coat with the panko mixture.
5. Place the cod fillets in the air fryer basket and spray with olive oil.
6. Cook for 15 minutes, flipping the cod halfway through.

Nutrition: Calories: 230 | Total Fat: 9g | Saturated Fat: 2g | Cholesterol: 70mg | Sodium: 390mg | Total Carbohydrates: 10g | Dietary Fiber: 1g | Protein: 25g

Crab Stuffed Salmon

Prep Time: 10 minutes | **Cook Time:** 20 minutes | **Serve:** 4

Ingredients:
- 4 (4-ounce) salmon fillets
- 1/2 cup crab meat
- 2 tablespoons light mayonnaise
- 2 tablespoons fresh parsley, chopped
- 1/4 teaspoon garlic powder
- 1/4 teaspoon onion powder
- 1/4 teaspoon paprika
- 1/4 teaspoon salt
- 1/4 teaspoon black pepper
- 2 tablespoons olive oil

Directions:
1. Preheat air fryer to 400 degrees F.
2. In a small bowl, mix together crab meat, mayonnaise, parsley, garlic powder, onion powder, paprika, salt, and pepper.
3. Place salmon fillets in a single layer in the air fryer.
4. Divide the crab mixture evenly among the salmon fillets, spreading it on top.
5. Drizzle the olive oil over the salmon and crab mixture.
6. Cook in the air fryer for 15-20 minutes, until the salmon is cooked through and the crab is golden brown.

Nutrition: Calories: 261 | Total Fat: 12g | Saturated Fat: 2g | Cholesterol: 62mg | Sodium: 441mg | Carbohydrates: 1g | Protein: 32g

Air Fried Salmon

Prep Time: 10 minutes | **Cook Time:** 15 minutes | Serves: 4

Ingredients:
- 4 (4-ounce) salmon fillets
- 2 tablespoons olive oil
- 2 tablespoons lemon juice
- 1 teaspoon garlic powder
- 1 teaspoon onion powder
- 1 teaspoon dried oregano
- 1/2 teaspoon paprika
- 1/2 teaspoon salt
- 1/4 teaspoon black pepper

Directions:
1. Preheat air fryer to 375°F.
2. Place salmon fillets in a shallow dish.
3. In a small bowl, whisk together olive oil, lemon juice, garlic powder, onion powder, oregano, paprika, salt, and pepper.
4. Pour the marinade over the salmon and let sit for 10 minutes.
5. Place the salmon in the air fryer basket and cook for 10-15 minutes, or until the salmon is cooked through.
6. Serve with your favorite side dish.

Nutrition: Calories: 240 | Total Fat: 13g | Saturated Fat: 2g | Cholesterol: 70mg | Sodium: 320mg | Carbohydrates: 1g | Protein: 25g

Crusted Mahi-Mahi

Prep Time: 10 minutes | **Cook Time:** 15 minutes | **Serve:** 4

Ingredients:
- 4 Mahi-Mahi fillets
- 2 tablespoons olive oil
- 2 tablespoons lemon juice
- 2 tablespoons Dijon mustard
- 1/2 cup crushed corn flakes
- 1/4 teaspoon garlic powder
- 1/4 teaspoon onion powder
- 1/4 teaspoon paprika
- Salt and pepper to taste

Directions:
1. Preheat air fryer to 400°F.
2. In a small bowl, mix together olive oil, lemon juice, and Dijon mustard.
3. In a separate bowl, mix together crushed corn flakes, garlic powder, onion powder, paprika, salt, and pepper.
4. Brush the mahi-mahi fillets with the olive oil mixture, then coat with the corn flake mixture.
5. Place the mahi-mahi fillets in the air fryer basket and cook for 15 minutes or until cooked through.
6. Serve with your favorite side dish.

Nutrition: Calories: 250 | Fat: 10g | Carbohydrates: 11g | Protein: 28g

Honey Tuna Steaks

Prep Time: 10 minutes | **Cook Time:** 15 minutes | **Serve:** 4

Ingredients:
- 4 tuna steaks, 4 ounces each
- 2 tablespoons olive oil
- 2 tablespoons honey
- 1 teaspoon garlic powder
- 1 teaspoon onion powder
- 1 teaspoon paprika
- 1/4 teaspoon black pepper
- Salt to taste

Directions:
1. Preheat the air fryer to 375°F.
2. In a small bowl, mix together the olive oil, honey, garlic powder, onion powder, paprika, black pepper, and salt.

3. Place the tuna steaks in the air fryer basket and brush with the honey mixture.
4. Cook for 10 minutes, flipping the steaks halfway through.
5. Remove from the air fryer and serve.

Nutrition: Calories: 224 | Total Fat: 9.3g | Saturated Fat: 1.3g | Cholesterol: 59mg | Sodium: 108mg | Carbohydrates: 5.7g | Fiber: 0.3g | Sugar: 5.3g | Protein: 28.3g

Salmon Cakes

Prep Time: 10 minutes | **Cook Time:** 10 minutes | **Serve:** 4

Ingredients:
- 2 cans of boneless and skinless salmon, drained
- 1/2 cup of finely chopped onion
- 1/4 cup of chopped fresh parsley
- 2 tablespoons of Dijon mustard
- 2 tablespoons of olive oil
- 2 tablespoons of lemon juice
- 1/2 cup of almond flour
- 1/2 teaspoon of garlic powder
- 1/4 teaspoon of black pepper
- 1/4 teaspoon of salt

Directions:
1. Preheat the air fryer to 350°F.
2. In a large bowl, combine the salmon, onion, parsley, mustard, olive oil, and lemon juice. Mix until well combined.
3. In a separate bowl, mix together the almond flour, garlic powder, black pepper, and salt.
4. Form the salmon mixture into 8 patties.
5. Dip each patty into the almond flour mixture, coating both sides.
6. Place the patties in the air fryer and cook for 10 minutes, flipping halfway through.

Nutrition: Calories: 177 | Fat: 10.4g | Carbs: 5.2g | Protein: 15.3g | Sodium: 437mg | Fiber: 1.4g

Crispy Fish Sticks

Prep Time: 10 minutes | **Cook Time:** 15 minutes | **Serve:** 4

Ingredients:
- 4 fish fillets, cut into sticks
- 1/4 cup whole wheat flour
- 1/4 cup cornstarch
- 1/2 teaspoon garlic powder
- 1/2 teaspoon onion powder

- 1/2 teaspoon paprika
- 1/2 teaspoon salt
- 1/4 teaspoon black pepper
- 1 egg, beaten
- 1/4 cup almond milk
- 1/2 cup panko breadcrumbs
- 2 tablespoons olive oil

Directions:
1. Preheat the air fryer to 400°F.
2. In a shallow bowl, combine the flour, cornstarch, garlic powder, onion powder, paprika, salt, and black pepper.
3. In a separate shallow bowl, whisk together the egg and almond milk.
4. Place the panko breadcrumbs in a third shallow bowl.
5. Dip each fish stick in the flour mixture, then the egg mixture, and finally the panko breadcrumbs.
6. Place the fish sticks in the air fryer basket and spray with the olive oil.
7. Cook for 15 minutes, flipping the fish sticks halfway through.

Nutrition: Calories: 240 | Fat: 8g | Protein: 19g | Carbs: 22g | Fiber: 2g | Sodium: 450mg

Honey-Glazed Salmon

Prep Time: 10 minutes | **Cook Time:** 15 minutes | **Serve:** 4

Ingredients:
- 4 salmon fillets
- 2 tablespoons olive oil
- 2 tablespoons honey
- 2 tablespoons lemon juice
- 2 tablespoons chopped fresh parsley
- 1 teaspoon garlic powder
- Salt and pepper to taste

Directions:
1. Preheat air fryer to 400°F.
2. Place salmon fillets in a shallow dish.
3. In a small bowl, mix together olive oil, honey, lemon juice, parsley, garlic powder, salt, and pepper.
4. Pour the mixture over the salmon and let marinate for 10 minutes.
5. Place the salmon in the air fryer basket and cook for 15 minutes.
6. Serve with a side of vegetables and enjoy.

Nutrition: Calories: 325 | Fat: 17g | Protein: 28g | Carbs: 10g | Fiber: 1g | Sugar: 8g

CHAPTER 6: SNACK RECIPES

Zucchini Fries

Prep Time: 10 minutes | **Cook Time:** 15 minutes | **Serve:** 4

Ingredients:
- 2 medium zucchini
- 2 tablespoons olive oil
- 1/2 teaspoon garlic powder
- 1/2 teaspoon paprika
- 1/4 teaspoon salt
- 1/4 teaspoon black pepper

Directions:
1. Preheat air fryer to 375°F.
2. Cut zucchini into fry shapes.
3. In a large bowl, combine zucchini, olive oil, garlic powder, paprika, salt, and pepper. Toss until zucchini is evenly coated.
4. Place zucchini in air fryer basket in a single layer.
5. Cook for 15 minutes, shaking basket halfway through.

Nutrition: Calories: 75 | Total Fat: 5g | Saturated Fat: 1g | Cholesterol: 0mg | Sodium: 160mg | Carbohydrates: 7g | Fiber: 2g | Sugar: 3g | Protein: 2g

Avocado Fries

Prep Time: 10 minutes | **Cook Time:** 15 minutes | **Serve:** 4

Ingredients:
- 2 medium avocados, peeled and sliced into 1/2-inch thick wedges
- 1/2 cup almond flour
- 1/4 cup grated Parmesan cheese
- 1 teaspoon garlic powder
- 1/2 teaspoon paprika
- 1/4 teaspoon salt
- 1/4 teaspoon black pepper
- 2 tablespoons olive oil

Directions:
1. Preheat air fryer to 400°F.
2. In a shallow bowl, combine almond flour, Parmesan cheese, garlic powder, paprika, salt and pepper.

3. Dip each avocado wedge into the almond flour mixture, coating evenly.
4. Place the avocado wedges in the air fryer basket and lightly spray with olive oil.
5. Cook for 10 minutes, flipping the wedges halfway through.
6. Serve with your favorite dipping sauce.

Nutrition: Calories: 153 | Total Fat: 11g | Saturated Fat: 2g | Cholesterol: 4mg | Sodium: 213mg | Carbohydrates: 10g | Fiber: 5g | Sugar: 1g | Protein: 5g

Roasted Peanut Butter Squash

Prep Time: 10 minutes | **Cook Time:** 25 minutes | **Serve:** 4

Ingredients:
- 2 medium squash, cut into cubes
- 2 tablespoons peanut butter
- 1 tablespoon olive oil
- 1 teaspoon garlic powder
- 1 teaspoon onion powder
- 1 teaspoon ground cumin
- 1 teaspoon smoked paprika
- Salt and pepper to taste

Directions:
1. Preheat air fryer to 400°F.
2. Place squash cubes in a large bowl.
3. In a small bowl, mix together peanut butter, olive oil, garlic powder, onion powder, cumin, and smoked paprika.
4. Pour the peanut butter mixture over the squash cubes and mix until all cubes are evenly coated.
5. Place the cubes in the air fryer basket and cook for 20-25 minutes, stirring halfway through.

Nutrition: Calories: 120 | Fat: 7g | Carbohydrates: 11g | Protein: 4g | Sodium: 50mg | Fiber: 3g

Roasted Chickpeas

Prep Time: 5 minutes | **Cook Time:** 20 minutes | **Serve:** 4

Ingredients:
- 2 cans of chickpeas, drained and rinsed
- 2 tablespoons olive oil
- 1 teaspoon garlic powder
- 1 teaspoon smoked paprika
- 1 teaspoon ground cumin
- 1 teaspoon onion powder
- Salt and pepper to taste

Directions:
1. Preheat the air fryer to 400 degrees F.
2. In a large bowl, combine the chickpeas, olive oil, garlic powder, smoked paprika, cumin, onion powder, salt and pepper. Toss to combine.
3. Place the chickpeas in the air fryer basket. Cook for 15-20 minutes, shaking the basket every 5 minutes.
4. When the chickpeas are golden brown and crispy, remove from the air fryer and serve.

Nutrition: Calories: 200 | Total Fat: 7g | Saturated Fat: 1g | Cholesterol: 0mg | Sodium: 5mg | Carbohydrates: 28g | Fiber: 7g | Sugar: 2g | Protein: 8g

Fried Spicy Green Beans

Prep Time: 10 minutes | **Cook Time:** 10 minutes | **Serve:** 4

Ingredients:
- 1 pound fresh green beans
- 2 tablespoons olive oil
- 1 teaspoon garlic powder
- 1 teaspoon chili powder
- 1/2 teaspoon cumin
- 1/2 teaspoon paprika
- Salt and pepper, to taste

Directions:
1. Preheat the air fryer to 400°F.
2. Trim the ends of the green beans and place them in a bowl.
3. Drizzle the olive oil over the green beans and toss to coat.
4. In a small bowl, mix together the garlic powder, chili powder, cumin, paprika, salt, and pepper.
5. Sprinkle the spice mixture over the green beans and toss to coat.
6. Place the green beans in the air fryer basket and cook for 10 minutes, shaking the basket halfway through.

Nutrition: Calories: 90 | Total Fat: 6g | Saturated Fat: 1g | Cholesterol: 0mg | Sodium: 73mg | Carbohydrates: 8g | Fiber: 3g | Sugar: 3g | Protein: 2g

Sweet Potato Nachos

Prep Time: 10 minutes | **Cook Time:** 15 minutes | **Serve:** 4

Ingredients:
- 2 medium sweet potatoes, peeled and cut into 1/4-inch slices
- 2 tablespoons olive oil
- 1/2 teaspoon garlic powder

- 1/2 teaspoon chili powder
- 1/4 teaspoon ground cumin
- 1/4 teaspoon paprika
- 1/4 teaspoon salt
- 1/4 cup shredded low-fat cheese
- 1/4 cup diced tomatoes
- 1/4 cup diced red onion
- 2 tablespoons chopped fresh cilantro
- 1/4 cup reduced-fat sour cream

Directions:
1. Preheat air fryer to 375°F.
2. Place sweet potato slices in a large bowl. Drizzle with olive oil and toss to coat.
3. In a small bowl, combine garlic powder, chili powder, cumin, paprika, and salt. Sprinkle over sweet potatoes and toss to coat.
4. Place sweet potatoes in a single layer in the air fryer basket. Cook for 15 minutes, flipping halfway through.
5. Remove sweet potatoes from the air fryer and place on a serving platter. Sprinkle with cheese, tomatoes, onion, and cilantro.
6. Serve with sour cream.

Nutrition: Calories: 140 | Total Fat: 7g | Saturated Fat: 2g | Cholesterol: 8mg | Sodium: 270mg | Carbohydrates: 15g | Fiber: 2g | Sugar: 4g | Protein: 5g

Rosemary-Garlic Brussels Sprouts

Prep Time: 10 minutes | **Cook Time:** 15 minutes | **Serve:** 4

Ingredients:
- 1 lb Brussels sprouts, trimmed and halved
- 2 tablespoons olive oil
- 2 cloves garlic, minced
- 1 teaspoon dried rosemary
- Salt and pepper to taste

Directions:
1. Preheat air fryer to 400°F.
2. Place Brussels sprouts in a bowl and add olive oil, garlic, rosemary, salt and pepper. Toss to combine.
3. Place Brussels sprouts in the air fryer basket and cook for 15 minutes, stirring halfway through.

Nutrition:
Calories: 115 | Total Fat: 7g | Saturated Fat: 1g | Cholesterol: 0mg | Sodium: 63mg | Carbohydrates: 11g | Fiber: 4g | Sugar: 3g | Protein: 4g

Buffalo Cauliflower

Prep Time: 10 minutes | **Cook Time:** 20 minutes | **Serve:** 4

Ingredients:
- 1 head of cauliflower, cut into florets
- 2 tablespoons olive oil
- 1/4 cup buffalo sauce
- 1/4 teaspoon garlic powder
- 1/4 teaspoon onion powder
- Salt and pepper, to taste

Directions:
1. Preheat air fryer to 400°F.
2. Place cauliflower florets in a large bowl. Drizzle with olive oil and toss to coat.
3. In a small bowl, mix together buffalo sauce, garlic powder, onion powder, salt and pepper.
4. Pour buffalo sauce mixture over cauliflower and toss to coat.
5. Place cauliflower in air fryer basket and cook for 15-20 minutes, shaking the basket every 5 minutes.
6. Serve hot with ranch dressing or blue cheese dressing.

Nutrition: Calories: 100 | Total Fat: 7g | Saturated Fat: 1g | Cholesterol: 0mg | Sodium: 590mg | Carbohydrates: 8g | Fiber: 3g | Sugar: 3g | Protein: 3g

Mini Pizza

Prep Time: 10 minutes | **Cook Time:** 10 minutes | **Serve:** 2

Ingredients:
- 2 whole wheat pitas
- 2 tablespoons of sugar-free pizza sauce
- 2 tablespoons of grated Parmesan cheese
- 2 tablespoons of low-fat mozzarella cheese
- 2 tablespoons of diced bell peppers
- 2 tablespoons of diced mushrooms
- 2 tablespoons of diced onions
- 2 tablespoons of diced tomatoes
- 1 tablespoon of olive oil
- Salt and pepper to taste

Directions:
1. Preheat the air fryer to 375°F.
2. Place the pitas on a cutting board and spread the pizza sauce over the top.

3. Sprinkle the Parmesan cheese, mozzarella cheese, bell peppers, mushrooms, onions, and tomatoes over the top of the pitas.
4. Drizzle the olive oil over the top of the pizzas.
5. Place the pizzas in the air fryer and cook for 10 minutes.
6. Remove the pizzas from the air fryer and season with salt and pepper to taste.

Nutrition: Calories: 210 | Total Fat: 8g | Saturated Fat: 2g | Cholesterol: 10mg | Sodium: 380mg | Carbohydrates: 24g | Fiber: 4g | Sugar: 3g | Protein: 9g

Egg Rolls

Prep Time: 10 minutes | **Cook Time:** 10 minutes | **Serve:** 4

Ingredients:
- 4 egg roll wrappers
- 1/2 cup cooked and shredded chicken
- 1/4 cup shredded carrots
- 1/4 cup shredded cabbage
- 2 tablespoons reduced-sodium soy sauce
- 1 tablespoon sesame oil
- 1/4 teaspoon garlic powder
- 1/4 teaspoon ground ginger
- Cooking spray

Directions:
1. Preheat air fryer to 375°F.
2. In a medium bowl, combine chicken, carrots, cabbage, soy sauce, sesame oil, garlic powder, and ginger. Stir to combine.
3. Place one egg roll wrapper on a clean work surface. Place about 2 tablespoons of the chicken mixture in the center of the wrapper. Fold the bottom corner of the wrapper up over the filling and tuck it under the filling. Fold the left and right corners in towards the center. Roll the wrapper up and away from you, making sure to keep the filling in place. Secure the top corner with a dab of water. Repeat with the remaining wrappers and filling.
4. Spray the egg rolls lightly with cooking spray. Place the egg rolls in the air fryer basket. Cook for 10 minutes, flipping halfway through.

Nutrition: Calories: 123 | Total Fat: 5g | Saturated Fat: 1g | Cholesterol: 25mg | Sodium: 545mg | Carbohydrates: 11g | Fiber: 1g | Sugar: 1g | Protein: 8g

Fish & Chips

Prep Time: 10 minutes | **Cook Time:** 15 minutes | **Serve:** 4

Ingredients:
- 4 (4-ounce) white fish fillets, such as cod or haddock
- 2 tablespoons olive oil
- 1/2 teaspoon garlic powder
- 1/2 teaspoon onion powder
- 1/2 teaspoon smoked paprika
- 1/4 teaspoon ground black pepper
- 2 tablespoons all-purpose flour
- 2 tablespoons cornstarch
- 1/2 teaspoon baking powder
- 1/4 teaspoon salt
- 1/2 cup cold water
- 2 cups air-popped popcorn

Directions:
1. Preheat air fryer to 400°F.
2. Place fish fillets on a plate and brush with olive oil. Sprinkle with garlic powder, onion powder, smoked paprika, and black pepper. Set aside.
3. In a medium bowl, whisk together flour, cornstarch, baking powder, and salt. Slowly add cold water and whisk until a thick batter forms.
4. Dip each fish fillet in the batter and then coat with air-popped popcorn. Place in the air fryer basket.
5. Cook for 8 minutes, flipping halfway through.
6. Serve with your favorite dipping sauce.

Nutrition: Calories: 250 | Fat: 8g | Protein: 22g | Carbohydrates: 19g | Fiber: 3g | Sodium: 360mg

Mozzarella Sticks

Prep Time: 10 minutes | **Cook Time:** 10 minutes | **Serve:** 4

Ingredients:
- 8 ounces of part-skim mozzarella cheese, cut into 12 sticks
- 2 tablespoons of all-purpose flour
- 1/4 teaspoon of garlic powder
- 1/4 teaspoon of onion powder
- 1/4 teaspoon of Italian seasoning
- 2 tablespoons of grated Parmesan cheese
- 1 large egg, lightly beaten
- 1/2 cup of panko breadcrumbs

- 2 tablespoons of olive oil

Directions:
1. Preheat the air fryer to 400 degrees F.
2. In a shallow bowl, combine the flour, garlic powder, onion powder, Italian seasoning, and Parmesan cheese.
3. In a separate shallow bowl, add the egg.
4. In a third shallow bowl, add the panko breadcrumbs.
5. Dip each mozzarella stick into the flour mixture, then into the egg, and finally into the panko breadcrumbs.
6. Place the mozzarella sticks into the air fryer and cook for 8-10 minutes, flipping halfway through.

Nutrition: Calories: 200 | Fat: 10g | Carbs: 10g | Protein: 15g

Eggplant Fries

Prep Time: 10 minutes | **Cook Time:** 20 minutes | **Serve:** 4

Ingredients:
- 2 large eggplants, cut into 1/4 inch slices
- 2 tablespoons olive oil
- 1 teaspoon garlic powder
- 1 teaspoon onion powder
- 1 teaspoon paprika
- Salt and pepper to taste

Directions:
1. Preheat air fryer to 400°F.
2. In a large bowl, combine eggplant slices with olive oil, garlic powder, onion powder, paprika, salt, and pepper. Toss to combine.
3. Place eggplant slices in the air fryer basket in a single layer.
4. Cook for 10 minutes, flipping halfway through.
5. Remove from air fryer and serve.

Nutrition: Calories: 90 | Total Fat: 5g | Saturated Fat: 1g | Cholesterol: 0mg | Sodium: 75mg | Carbohydrates: 10g | Fiber: 3g | Sugar: 5g | Protein: 2g

Carrot Fries

Prep Time: 10 minutes | **Cook Time:** 15 minutes | **Serve:** 4

Ingredients:
- 1 lb. carrots, peeled and cut into thin strips
- 2 tablespoons olive oil

- 1 teaspoon garlic powder
- 1 teaspoon onion powder
- 1 teaspoon paprika
- Salt and pepper to taste

Directions:
1. Preheat air fryer to 375°F.
2. In a large bowl, combine carrots, olive oil, garlic powder, onion powder, paprika, salt, and pepper. Toss to coat.
3. Place carrots in air fryer basket in a single layer. Cook for 10 minutes, shaking basket halfway through.
4. Increase heat to 400°F and cook for an additional 5 minutes, or until carrots are golden brown and crispy.

Nutrition: Calories: 127 | Total Fat: 7g | Saturated Fat: 1g | Sodium: 140mg | Carbohydrates: 14g | Fiber: 4g | Protein: 2g

Kale Chips with Lemon Yogurt Sauce

Prep Time: 10 minutes | **Cook Time:** 15 minutes | **Serve:** 4

Ingredients:
- 2 bunches of kale, washed and dried
- 2 tablespoons olive oil
- 1 teaspoon garlic powder
- 1 teaspoon onion powder
- 1/2 teaspoon sea salt
- 1/4 teaspoon black pepper
- 1/2 cup plain Greek yogurt
- 2 tablespoons lemon juice
- 1 tablespoon honey
- 1/4 teaspoon garlic powder
- 1/4 teaspoon onion powder

Directions:
1. Preheat air fryer to 350°F.
2. Cut the kale leaves into 2-inch pieces, discarding the thick stems. Place the kale pieces in a large bowl.
3. Drizzle the olive oil over the kale and add the garlic powder, onion powder, sea salt, and black pepper. Toss to coat.
4. Place the kale pieces in the air fryer basket in an even layer. Cook for 10 minutes, shaking the basket halfway through.
5. In a small bowl, combine the Greek yogurt, lemon juice, honey, garlic powder, and onion powder. Stir to combine.

6. Serve the kale chips with the lemon yogurt sauce.

Nutrition: Calories: 115 | Total Fat: 6 g | Saturated Fat: 1 g | Cholesterol: 3 mg | Sodium: 221 mg | Carbohydrates: 11 g | Fiber: 2 g | Sugar: 6 g | Protein: 5 g

Basil Pesto Bruschetta

Prep Time: 10 minutes | **Cook Time:** 10 minutes | **Serve:** 4

Ingredients:
- 2 cups fresh basil leaves
- 2 cloves garlic, minced
- 2 tablespoons olive oil
- 2 tablespoons grated Parmesan cheese
- 2 tablespoons pine nuts
- 1/4 teaspoon salt
- 1/4 teaspoon freshly ground black pepper
- 4 slices whole wheat bread
- 1/4 cup diced tomatoes
- 2 tablespoons shredded mozzarella cheese

Directions:
1. In a food processor, combine the basil, garlic, olive oil, Parmesan cheese, pine nuts, salt, and pepper. Pulse until the mixture is smooth.
2. Place the bread slices in the air fryer and cook for 5 minutes at 350°F.
3. Spread the pesto on the toasted bread slices. Top with the diced tomatoes and mozzarella cheese.
4. Place the bruschetta back in the air fryer and cook for an additional 5 minutes at 350°F.
5. Serve the bruschetta warm.

Nutrition: Calories: 210 | Total Fat: 11g | Saturated Fat: 3g | Cholesterol: 10mg | Sodium: 350mg | Carbohydrates: 21g | Fiber: 3g | Sugar: 2g | Protein: 8g

Cinnamon Pear Chips

Prep Time: 10 minutes | **Cook Time:** 15 minutes | **Serve:** 4

Ingredients:
- 4 pears, thinly sliced
- 2 tablespoons ground cinnamon
- 2 tablespoons coconut sugar
- 2 tablespoons olive oil
- Pinch of salt

Directions:
1. Preheat air fryer to 350°F.
2. In a medium bowl, combine the pears, cinnamon, coconut sugar, olive oil, and salt. Toss until the pears are evenly coated.
3. Place the pears in the air fryer basket in a single layer.
4. Cook for 15 minutes, shaking the basket halfway through.
5. Remove from the air fryer and let cool before serving.

Nutrition: Calories: 98 | Fat: 4g | Carbohydrates: 16g | Protein: 1g | Sodium: 4mg | Fiber: 3g

Phyllo Vegetable Triangles

Prep Time: 10 minutes | **Cook Time:** 20 minutes | **Serve:** 4

Ingredients:
- 2 tablespoons olive oil
- 1/2 cup diced onion
- 1/2 cup diced bell pepper
- 1/2 cup diced zucchini
- 1/2 cup diced mushrooms
- 1/2 teaspoon garlic powder
- 1/4 teaspoon black pepper
- 1/4 teaspoon salt
- 1/2 cup shredded mozzarella cheese
- 1/2 cup crumbled feta cheese
- 8 sheets phyllo dough
- 2 tablespoons butter, melted

Directions:
1. Preheat the air fryer to 375°F.
2. Heat the olive oil in a skillet over medium heat. Add the onion, bell pepper, zucchini, mushrooms, garlic powder, black pepper, and salt. Cook for 5 minutes, stirring occasionally.
3. In a bowl, mix together the cooked vegetables, mozzarella cheese, and feta cheese.
4. Cut each sheet of phyllo dough into 4 equal pieces. Place a spoonful of the vegetable mixture onto each piece of phyllo dough. Fold the dough into triangles, sealing the edges with melted butter.
5. Place the triangles in the air fryer basket and cook for 10 minutes, flipping halfway through.

Nutrition: Calories: 166 | Fat: 10g | Carbohydrates: 11g | Protein: 8g | Sodium: 456mg | Fiber: 1g

CHAPTER 7: DESSERTS RECIPES

Chocolate Brownies

Prep Time: 10 minutes | **Cook Time:** 20 minutes | **Serve:** 8

Ingredients:
- 1/2 cup all-purpose flour
- 1/4 cup cocoa powder
- 1/4 teaspoon baking powder
- 1/4 teaspoon salt
- 1/2 cup sugar-free sweetener
- 1/4 cup vegetable oil
- 2 eggs
- 2 tablespoons unsweetened applesauce
- 1 teaspoon vanilla extract
- 1/2 cup semi-sweet chocolate chips

Directions:
1. Preheat air fryer to 350°F.
2. In a large bowl, whisk together the flour, cocoa powder, baking powder, and salt.
3. In a separate bowl, whisk together the sugar-free sweetener, vegetable oil, eggs, applesauce, and vanilla extract.
4. Pour the wet ingredients into the dry ingredients and mix until just combined.
5. Fold in the chocolate chips.
6. Grease an 8x8-inch baking pan with non-stick cooking spray.
7. Pour the batter into the pan and spread it evenly.
8. Place the pan in the air fryer and cook for 20 minutes.
9. Let cool before cutting into squares.

Nutrition: Calories: 135 | Total Fat: 8.5g | Saturated Fat: 3.5g | Cholesterol: 38mg | Sodium: 75mg | Carbohydrates: 13.5g | Fiber: 1.5g | Sugar: 5g | Protein: 2.5g

Spiced Apples

Prep Time: 10 minutes | **Cook Time:** 10 minutes | **Serve:** 4

Ingredients:
4 apples, cored and cut into wedges
1 teaspoon ground cinnamon
1/4 teaspoon ground nutmeg
1/4 teaspoon ground ginger
1/4 teaspoon ground allspice

1/4 teaspoon ground cloves
1/4 teaspoon ground cardamom
1 tablespoon honey
1 tablespoon olive oil

Directions:
1. Preheat the air fryer to 350°F.
2. Place the apple wedges in a large bowl.
3. In a small bowl, mix together the cinnamon, nutmeg, ginger, allspice, cloves, and cardamom.
4. Sprinkle the spice mixture over the apples and toss to coat.
5. Drizzle the honey and olive oil over the apples and toss to coat.
6. Place the apples in the air fryer basket and cook for 10 minutes, shaking the basket halfway through.

Nutrition: Calories: 120 | Total Fat: 4g | Saturated Fat: 1g | Cholesterol: 0mg | Sodium: 0mg | Carbohydrates: 21g | Dietary Fiber: 4g | Sugars: 15g | Protein: 1g

Sweet Potato Fries

Prep Time: 10 minutes | **Cook Time:** 15 minutes | **Serve:** 4

Ingredients:
- 2 large sweet potatoes, peeled and cut into 1/4-inch thick fries
- 2 tablespoons olive oil
- 1 teaspoon garlic powder
- 1 teaspoon paprika
- 1/2 teaspoon salt
- 1/4 teaspoon black pepper

Directions:
1. Preheat air fryer to 400°F.
2. Place sweet potato fries in a large bowl and drizzle with olive oil.
3. Add garlic powder, paprika, salt, and black pepper and toss to combine.
4. Place fries in the air fryer basket in a single layer, making sure not to overcrowd.
5. Cook for 10 minutes, shaking the basket halfway through.
6. Increase the temperature to 425°F and cook for an additional 5 minutes, or until golden brown and crispy.

Nutrition: Calories: 153 | Total Fat: 7g | Saturated Fat: 1g | Cholesterol: 0mg | Sodium: 330mg | Carbohydrates: 21g | Fiber: 3g | Sugar: 4g | Protein: 2g

Chocolate Lava Cake

Prep Time: 10 minutes | **Cook Time:** 20 minutes | **Serve:** 4

Ingredients:
- 1/2 cup all-purpose flour
- 1/4 cup cocoa powder
- 1/4 teaspoon baking powder
- 1/4 teaspoon salt
- 1/4 cup granulated sugar substitute
- 2 tablespoons butter, melted
- 1/4 cup low-fat milk
- 1 teaspoon vanilla extract
- 1/4 cup semi-sweet chocolate chips

Directions:
1. Preheat the air fryer to 350°F.
2. In a medium bowl, whisk together the flour, cocoa powder, baking powder, salt, and sugar substitute.
3. In a separate bowl, mix together the melted butter, milk, and vanilla extract.
4. Add the wet ingredients to the dry ingredients and mix until just combined.
5. Stir in the chocolate chips.
6. Grease a 4-inch round cake pan with non-stick cooking spray and pour the batter into the pan.
7. Place the cake pan in the air fryer and cook for 20 minutes.
8. Allow the cake to cool for 5 minutes before serving.

Nutrition: Calories: 125 | Total Fat: 6g | Saturated Fat: 4g | Cholesterol: 10mg | Sodium: 140mg | Carbohydrates: 15g | Fiber: 2g | Sugar: 4g | Protein: 3g

Chocolate Donuts

Prep Time: 10 minutes | **Cook Time:** 8 minutes | **Serve:** 6

Ingredients:
- 1 cup all-purpose flour
- 1/4 cup cocoa powder
- 1 teaspoon baking powder
- 1/4 teaspoon baking soda
- 1/4 teaspoon salt
- 1/2 cup granulated sugar substitute
- 1/2 cup unsweetened almond milk
- 2 tablespoons vegetable oil
- 1 teaspoon pure vanilla extract
- 1/4 cup sugar-free chocolate chips

Directions:
1. Preheat the air fryer to 350°F.
2. In a medium bowl, whisk together the flour, cocoa powder, baking powder, baking soda, and salt.
3. In a separate bowl, whisk together the sugar substitute, almond milk, vegetable oil, and vanilla extract.
4. Add the wet ingredients to the dry ingredients and mix until just combined. Fold in the chocolate chips.
5. Grease the air fryer basket with nonstick cooking spray.
6. Using a tablespoon, scoop the batter into the air fryer basket. Cook for 8 minutes, or until the donuts are cooked through.

Nutrition: Calories: 130 | Fat: 6g | Carbohydrates: 16g | Protein: 2g | Fiber: 2g | Sugar: 0g

Peanut Butter Cookies

Prep Time: 10 minutes | **Cook Time:** 10 minutes | Serves: 12

Ingredients:
- 2/3 cup natural peanut butter
- 2 tablespoons coconut oil
- 1/2 cup coconut sugar
- 1 teaspoon vanilla extract
- 1/2 teaspoon baking soda
- 1/4 teaspoon sea salt
- 1 large egg
- 1/4 cup oat flour

Directions:
1. Preheat your air fryer to 350°F.
2. In a medium bowl, combine the peanut butter, coconut oil, coconut sugar, vanilla extract, baking soda, and sea salt. Stir until combined.
3. Add the egg and mix until combined.
4. Add the oat flour and mix until combined.
5. Using a tablespoon, scoop out 12 balls of dough and place them on a parchment-lined baking sheet.
6. Place the baking sheet in the air fryer and cook for 8-10 minutes, or until golden brown.
7. Remove from the air fryer and let cool before serving.

Nutrition: Calories: 101 | Fat: 6.4g | Carbohydrates: 9.3g | Protein: 2.7g | Fiber: 1.3g | Sugar: 5.3g

Cheesecake Bites

Prep Time: 10 minutes | **Cook Time:** 15 minutes | **Serve:** 8

Ingredients:
- 2 packages of reduced-fat cream cheese, softened
- 1/2 cup granulated sugar substitute
- 2 eggs
- 1 teaspoon vanilla extract
- 1/4 teaspoon ground cinnamon
- 1/4 cup graham cracker crumbs
- 2 tablespoons melted butter
- 1/4 cup sugar-free raspberry jam

Directions:
1. Preheat the air fryer to 350°F.
2. In a medium bowl, beat the cream cheese and sugar substitute until smooth.
3. Add the eggs, vanilla extract, and cinnamon and mix until combined.
4. In a separate bowl, mix the graham cracker crumbs and melted butter until combined.
5. Line a baking sheet with parchment paper.
6. Scoop 1 tablespoon of the cream cheese mixture onto the parchment paper.
7. Top each scoop with 1 teaspoon of the raspberry jam.
8. Top each scoop with 1 teaspoon of the graham cracker crumb mixture.
9. Place the baking sheet in the air fryer and cook for 15 minutes.
10. Allow the cheesecake bites to cool before serving.

Nutrition: Calories: 110 | Fat: 7g | Carbohydrates: 8g | Protein: 4g | Sodium: 140mg | Fiber: 0g

Chocolate Cake

Prep Time: 10 minutes | **Cook Time:** 25 minutes | **Serve:** 8

Ingredients:
- 2 cups all-purpose flour
- 1/2 cup cocoa powder
- 1 teaspoon baking powder
- 1 teaspoon baking soda
- 1/2 teaspoon salt
- 1/2 cup granulated sugar
- 1/2 cup light brown sugar
- 1/2 cup vegetable oil
- 2 large eggs
- 1 teaspoon vanilla extract
- 1/2 cup low-fat buttermilk

- 1/2 cup semi-sweet chocolate chips

Directions:
1. Preheat the air fryer to 350°F. Grease an 8-inch round cake pan with nonstick cooking spray.
2. In a medium bowl, whisk together the flour, cocoa powder, baking powder, baking soda, and salt.
3. In a large bowl, whisk together the sugars, oil, eggs, and vanilla extract until combined.
4. Add the dry ingredients to the wet ingredients and whisk until combined.
5. Add the buttermilk and whisk until combined.
6. Fold in the chocolate chips.
7. Pour the batter into the prepared pan and place in the air fryer. Cook for 25 minutes or until a toothpick inserted into the center comes out clean.
8. Allow the cake to cool in the pan for 10 minutes before transferring to a wire rack to cool completely.

Nutrition: Calories: 210 | Fat: 9g | Carbohydrates: 28g | Protein: 3g | Fiber: 1g | Sodium: 150mg

Grain-free Molten Lava Cakes

Prep Time: 10 minutes | **Cook Time:** 10 minutes | **Serve:** 4

Ingredients:
- 1/2 cup almond flour
- 1/4 cup coconut flour
- 1/4 cup cocoa powder
- 1/4 teaspoon baking powder
- 1/4 teaspoon salt
- 1/4 cup coconut sugar
- 2 eggs
- 2 tablespoons coconut oil, melted
- 1/2 teaspoon vanilla extract
- 1/4 cup dark chocolate chips

Directions:
1. Preheat air fryer to 350°F.
2. In a medium bowl, whisk together almond flour, coconut flour, cocoa powder, baking powder, salt, and coconut sugar.
3. In a separate bowl, whisk together eggs, coconut oil, and vanilla extract.
4. Add wet ingredients to dry ingredients and mix until combined.
5. Fold in chocolate chips.
6. Grease 4 ramekins with coconut oil. Divide batter evenly among ramekins.
7. Place ramekins in air fryer and cook for 10 minutes.
8. Let cool for 5 minutes before serving.

Nutrition: Calories: 190 | Fat: 11g | Carbs: 20g | Protein: 5g | Fiber: 4g | Sugar: 12g

Tahini-Crusted Chicken

Prep Time: 10 minutes | **Cook Time:** 15 minutes | **Serve:** 4

Ingredients:
4 boneless, skinless chicken breasts
1/2 cup tahini
1/4 cup almond meal
1/2 teaspoon garlic powder
1/2 teaspoon onion powder
1/2 teaspoon paprika
1/2 teaspoon salt
1/4 teaspoon black pepper

Directions:
1. Preheat air fryer to 400°F.
2. In a shallow bowl, combine tahini, almond meal, garlic powder, onion powder, paprika, salt, and pepper.
3. Dip chicken breasts in tahini mixture, coating both sides.
4. Place chicken breasts in air fryer basket.
5. Cook for 15 minutes, flipping halfway through.

Nutrition: Calories: 310 | Fat: 16g | Protein: 31g | Carbs: 8g | Fiber: 3g | Sugar: 2g

Oatmeal Chocolate Chunk Cookies

Prep Time: 10 minutes | **Cook Time:** 10 minutes | **Serve:** 24 cookies

Ingredients:
- 2 cups old-fashioned oats
- 1/2 cup almond flour
- 1/4 cup coconut sugar
- 1/4 teaspoon baking soda
- 1/4 teaspoon salt
- 1/2 cup coconut oil, melted
- 1/4 cup maple syrup
- 1 teaspoon vanilla extract
- 1/2 cup dark chocolate chunks

Directions:
1. Preheat air fryer to 350°F.
2. In a medium bowl, whisk together oats, almond flour, coconut sugar, baking soda, and salt.
3. In a separate bowl, whisk together coconut oil, maple syrup, and vanilla extract.
4. Add wet ingredients to dry ingredients and stir until combined.

5. Fold in chocolate chunks.
6. Scoop dough into 1-inch balls and place in air fryer.
7. Cook for 10 minutes, flipping halfway through.
8. Allow to cool before serving.

Nutrition: Calories: 120 | Fat: 7g | Carbs: 13g | Protein: 2g | Fiber: 2g

Eggless & Vegan Air Fryer Cake

Prep Time: 10 minutes | **Cook Time:** 15 minutes | **Serve:** 8

Ingredients:
- 1 cup all-purpose flour
- 1 teaspoon baking powder
- 1/4 teaspoon baking soda
- 1/4 teaspoon salt
- 1/2 cup coconut oil
- 1/2 cup almond milk
- 1/2 cup applesauce
- 1 teaspoon vanilla extract
- 1/2 cup sugar-free sweetener
- 1/2 cup sugar-free chocolate chips

Directions:
1. Preheat the air fryer to 350°F.
2. In a medium bowl, mix together the flour, baking powder, baking soda, and salt.
3. In a separate bowl, whisk together the coconut oil, almond milk, applesauce, vanilla extract, and sugar-free sweetener.
4. Add the wet ingredients to the dry ingredients and mix until just combined.
5. Fold in the chocolate chips.
6. Grease an 8-inch round cake pan with cooking spray and pour the batter into the pan.
7. Place the cake pan in the air fryer and cook for 15 minutes.
8. Allow the cake to cool before serving.

Nutrition: Calories: 160 | Total Fat: 11g | Saturated Fat: 8g | Trans Fat: 0g | Cholesterol: 0mg | Sodium: 140mg | Carbohydrates: 14g | Fiber: 1g | Sugar: 6g | Protein: 2g

Apple Cider Vinegar Donuts

Prep Time: 10 minutes | **Cook Time:** 10 minutes | **Serve:** 6

Ingredients:
-1/2 cup all-purpose flour
-1/4 cup almond flour

-1/4 cup coconut sugar
-1 teaspoon baking powder
-1/4 teaspoon baking soda
-1/4 teaspoon ground cinnamon
-1/4 teaspoon ground nutmeg
-1/4 teaspoon salt
-1/4 cup unsweetened applesauce
-1/4 cup apple cider vinegar
-1/4 cup almond milk
-1 teaspoon vanilla extract
-1 tablespoon melted coconut oil

Directions:
1. Preheat air fryer to 350°F.
2. In a medium bowl, whisk together the all-purpose flour, almond flour, coconut sugar, baking powder, baking soda, cinnamon, nutmeg, and salt.
3. In a separate bowl, whisk together the applesauce, apple cider vinegar, almond milk, vanilla extract, and melted coconut oil.
4. Add the wet ingredients to the dry ingredients and stir until just combined.
5. Grease the air fryer basket with non-stick cooking spray.
6. Using a spoon, drop the batter into the air fryer basket, making sure to leave some space between each donut.
7. Cook for 8-10 minutes, or until the donuts are golden brown and cooked through.
8. Allow the donuts to cool before serving.

Nutrition: Calories: 130 | Total Fat: 4g | Saturated Fat: 2g | Cholesterol: 0mg | Sodium: 170mg | Carbohydrates: 21g | Fiber: 2g | Sugar: 8g | Protein: 3g

Molten Lava Mug Cake

Prep Time: 5 minutes | **Cook Time:** 8 minutes | **Serve:** 1

Ingredients:
2 tablespoons almond flour
1 tablespoon coconut flour
1 tablespoon cocoa powder
2 tablespoons granulated erythritol sweetener
1/4 teaspoon baking powder
1/4 teaspoon baking soda
Pinch of salt
2 tablespoons melted butter
1 large egg
1 teaspoon vanilla extract
2 tablespoons sugar-free chocolate chips

Directions:
1. In a small bowl, mix together almond flour, coconut flour, cocoa powder, erythritol, baking powder, baking soda, and salt.
2. In a separate bowl, whisk together melted butter, egg, and vanilla extract.
3. Add dry ingredients to wet ingredients and mix until combined.
4. Stir in chocolate chips.
5. Grease a mug with butter or cooking spray.
6. Pour batter into mug and place in air fryer.
7. Cook at 350°F for 8 minutes.

Nutrition: Calories: 250 | Total Fat: 19g | Saturated Fat: 11g | Cholesterol: 105mg | Sodium: 250mg | Total Carbohydrates: 13g | Dietary Fiber: 5g | Sugars: 2g | Protein: 8g

Coconut Flour Mug Cake

Prep Time: 5 minutes | **Cook Time:** 8 minutes | **Serve:** 1

Ingredients:
- 2 tablespoons coconut flour
- 2 tablespoons unsweetened almond milk
- 1 tablespoon coconut oil
- 1 teaspoon baking powder
- 1/2 teaspoon vanilla extract
- 1/4 teaspoon ground cinnamon
- 2 tablespoons granulated sugar substitute
- Pinch of salt

Directions:
1. In a medium bowl, mix together the coconut flour, baking powder, cinnamon, sugar substitute, and salt.
2. Add the almond milk, coconut oil, and vanilla extract and mix until combined.
3. Grease an 8-inch round air fryer basket with cooking spray.
4. Pour the batter into the air fryer basket and spread evenly.
5. Cook at 350°F for 8 minutes.
6. Let cool for a few minutes before serving.

Nutrition: Calories: 145 | Carbohydrates: 11g | Protein: 3g | Fat: 11g | Sodium: 140mg | Sugar: 0g

Mini Cheesecakes

Prep Time: 10 minutes | **Cook Time:** 20 minutes | Serves: 12

Ingredients:
- 2 packages (8 oz each) reduced-fat cream cheese, softened
- 1/2 cup granulated sugar
- 2 large eggs
- 2 teaspoons vanilla extract
- 12 reduced-fat graham cracker sheets, crushed
- 1/4 cup melted butter
- 2 tablespoons sugar-free strawberry jam

Directions:
1. Preheat air fryer to 350°F.
2. In a large bowl, beat cream cheese and sugar until smooth. Beat in eggs and vanilla until blended.
3. In a separate bowl, combine graham cracker crumbs, melted butter, and sugar-free jam. Mix until combined.
4. Place 12 paper cupcake liners in a muffin tin. Divide graham cracker mixture evenly among liners.
5. Divide cream cheese mixture evenly among liners.
6. Place muffin tin in air fryer and cook for 20 minutes.

Nutrition: Calories: 150 | Fat: 9g | Carbohydrates: 14g | Protein: 4g | Fiber: 1g | Sugar: 8g

Coconut Macaroons

Prep Time: 10 minutes | **Cook Time:** 10 minutes | Serves: 12

Ingredients:
- 2 cups unsweetened shredded coconut
- 2 tablespoons coconut flour
- 2 tablespoons honey
- 2 tablespoons coconut oil
- 1 teaspoon vanilla extract
- 2 egg whites
- Pinch of salt

Directions:
1. Preheat air fryer to 350°F.
2. In a medium bowl, mix together the shredded coconut, coconut flour, honey, coconut oil, vanilla extract, egg whites, and salt.
3. Form the mixture into 12 small mounds and place them in the air fryer basket.
4. Cook for 10 minutes, flipping the macaroons halfway through.
5. Remove from the air fryer and let cool before serving.

Nutrition: Calories: 70 | Fat: 5g | Carbs: 6g | Protein: 1g | Sodium: 40mg | Sugar: 4g

Coconut Pie Air Fryer Recipe

Prep Time: 10 minutes | **Cook Time:** 20 minutes | **Serve:** 8

Ingredients:
- 1/2 cup all-purpose flour
- 1/4 cup sugar-free sweetener
- 1/4 teaspoon salt
- 1/4 cup cold butter, cut into small pieces
- 1 large egg
- 1/4 cup unsweetened coconut flakes
- 1/4 cup sugar-free condensed milk
- 1/4 cup sugar-free coconut flakes
- 1/4 cup sugar-free shredded coconut
- 1/4 teaspoon ground cinnamon

Directions:
1. Preheat the air fryer to 350 degrees F.
2. In a medium bowl, combine the flour, sweetener, and salt. Cut in the butter with a pastry blender or two knives until the mixture resembles coarse crumbs. Add the egg and mix until the dough comes together.
3. Press the dough into a 9-inch pie plate. Bake in the preheated air fryer for 10 minutes.
4. In a medium bowl, combine the coconut flakes, condensed milk, shredded coconut, and cinnamon. Pour the mixture into the pre-baked crust.
5. Bake in the preheated air fryer for 10 minutes. Let cool before serving.

Nutrition: Calories: 95 | Total Fat: 5g | Saturated Fat: 3g | Cholesterol: 20mg | Sodium: 90mg | Carbohydrates: 11g | Fiber: 1g | Sugar: 2g | Protein: 2g

Crustless Cheesecake

Prep Time: 10 minutes | **Cook Time:** 30 minutes | **Serves:** 8

Ingredients:
- 2 (8 oz) packages of cream cheese, softened
- 2 eggs
- 1/4 cup of sugar substitute
- 1 teaspoon of vanilla extract
- 1/4 teaspoon of salt
- 1/4 cup of heavy cream
- 2 tablespoons of all-purpose flour

Directions:
1. Preheat the air fryer to 350°F.
2. In a large bowl, beat the cream cheese until smooth.
3. Add the eggs, sugar substitute, vanilla extract, salt, heavy cream, and flour. Beat until combined.
4. Pour the mixture into a greased 9-inch round cake pan.
5. Place the cake pan in the air fryer and cook for 30 minutes.
6. Let the cheesecake cool before serving.

Nutrition: Calories: 150 | Total Fat: 10g | Saturated Fat: 6g | Cholesterol: 70mg | Sodium: 200mg | Carbohydrates: 8g | Fiber: 0g | Sugar: 3g | Protein: 4g

Low-Sugar Blueberry Cupcakes

Prep Time: 10 minutes | **Cook Time:** 15 minutes | **Serve:** 12 cupcakes

Ingredients:
- 2 cups all-purpose flour
- 1 teaspoon baking powder
- 1/2 teaspoon baking soda
- 1/4 teaspoon salt
- 1/2 cup unsalted butter, softened
- 1/2 cup granulated sugar substitute
- 2 large eggs
- 1 teaspoon vanilla extract
- 1/2 cup low-fat buttermilk
- 1 cup fresh blueberries

Directions:
1. Preheat the air fryer to 350°F. Grease a 12-cup muffin tin with cooking spray.
2. In a medium bowl, whisk together the flour, baking powder, baking soda, and salt.
3. In a large bowl, beat the butter and sugar substitute with an electric mixer until light and fluffy. Beat in the eggs, one at a time, then stir in the vanilla.
4. Add the flour mixture and buttermilk alternately to the butter mixture, stirring just until combined. Gently fold in the blueberries.
5. Divide the batter evenly among the prepared muffin cups. Bake in the air fryer for 15 minutes, or until a toothpick inserted in the center of a cupcake comes out clean.
6. Let the cupcakes cool in the pan for 10 minutes before transferring to a wire rack to cool completely.

Nutrition: Calories: 128 | Total Fat: 6g | Saturated Fat: 3g | Cholesterol: 37mg | Sodium: 135mg | Carbohydrates: 16g | Fiber: 1g | Sugar: 2g | Protein: 3g

Peach Cobbler

Prep Time: 10 minutes | **Cook Time:** 20 minutes | Serves: 4

Ingredients:
- 4 cups of fresh or frozen peaches, peeled and sliced
- 1/4 cup of granulated sugar substitute
- 2 tablespoons of cornstarch
- 1 teaspoon of ground cinnamon
- 1/4 teaspoon of ground nutmeg
- 1/4 teaspoon of ground ginger
- 1/4 teaspoon of salt
- 1/2 cup of all-purpose flour
- 1/2 cup of rolled oats
- 1/2 cup of brown sugar substitute
- 1/2 cup of butter, melted
- 1 teaspoon of vanilla extract

Directions:
1. Preheat the air fryer to 350°F.
2. In a medium bowl, combine the peaches, sugar substitute, cornstarch, cinnamon, nutmeg, ginger, and salt. Mix until the peaches are evenly coated.
3. In a separate bowl, combine the flour, oats, brown sugar substitute, melted butter, and vanilla extract. Mix until the ingredients are evenly combined.
4. Place the peach mixture into a greased air fryer-safe dish. Top with the oat mixture.
5. Place the dish into the air fryer and cook for 15-20 minutes, or until the topping is golden brown and the peaches are tender.

Nutrition: Calories: 195 | Carbohydrates: 25g | Protein: 2g | Fat: 10g | Saturated Fat: 6g | Cholesterol: 20mg | Sodium: 140mg | Potassium: 137mg | Fiber: 2g | Sugar: 9g | Vitamin A: 545IU | Vitamin C: 5.4mg | Calcium: 28mg | Iron: 0.9mg

30 DAYS MEAL PLAN

B. Breakfast **L.** Lunch **D.** Dinner

Day 1
B. Asparagus Omelet
L. Chicken Drumsticks
D. Breaded Cod

Day 2
B. Egg Bites
L. Low-Carb Chicken Meatballs
D. Lemon Chili Salmon

Day 3
B. Morning Sausage Patties
L. Herbed Lamb Chops
D. Steak Wrapped Asparagus

Day 4
B. Fried Egg
L. Low-Fat Steak
D. Crusted Mahi-Mahi

Day 5
B. Banana Muffins
L. Chicken Tikka Kebab
D. Roasted Bell Peppers

Day 6
B. Herb Frittata
L. Chicken Wings with Alfredo Sauce
D. Salmon Cakes

Day 7
B. Breakfast Cookies
L. Garlic Butter Steaks
D. Cilantro Lime Shrimps

Day 8
B. Phyllo Vegetable Triangles
L. Basil Pesto Bruschetta
D. Crispy Fish Sticks

Day 9
B. Scallion Sandwich
L. Double Cheeseburger
D. Lemon Pepper Shrimp

Day 10
B. Tofu Scramble
L. Broccoli Chicken Casserole
D. Salmon Cakes with Sriracha Mayo

Day 11
B. Baked Eggs
L. Roasted Vegetable and Chicken Salad
D. Crumbed Fish

Day 12
B. Pumpkin Pie French Toast
L. Greek Lemon Chicken
D. Air Fried Tofu

Day 13
B. Spinach and Tomato Frittata
L. Meatloaf
D. Turkey Patties

Day 14
B. Tasty Chicken Patties
L. Buffalo Chicken Hot Wings
D. Vegetarian Fajitas

Day 15
B. Grilled Cheese
L. Chicken Schnitzel
D. Rainbow Vegetable Fritters

Day 16
B. Santa Fe Style Pizza
L. Crusted Chicken Drumsticks
D. Corn on the Cob with Herb Butter

Day 17
B. Scrambled Egg
L. Beef Schnitzel
D. Crispy Blooming Onion

Day 18
B. Egg Croquettes
L. Japanese Chicken Tenders
D. Classic Fried Pickles

Day 19
B. Breakfast Cheese Bread Cups
L. Beef Korma Curry
D. Coconut Shrimp
Day 20
B. Air Fried Pickles
L. Air Fryer Chicken Cutlets
D. Honey-Glazed Salmon
Day 21
B. Grilled Sandwich With Three Types Of Cheese
L. Crispy Tofu In Asian Sauce
D. Tuna Burgers
Day 22
B. Zucchini Pizza
L. Cracker Barrel Meatloaf
D. Honey Tuna Steaks
Day 23
B. Mozzarella Sticks
L. Meatloaf Slider Wraps
D. Shrimp Scampi
Day 24
B. Fried Okra
L. Family Vegetable Gratin
D. Fried Peppers with Sriracha Mayo
Day 25
B. Garlic-Roasted Bell Peppers
L. Beef Curry
D. Lobster Tails with Garlic-Lemon Butter
Day 26
B. Sweet Corn Fritters with Avocado
L. Lemon Pepper Chicken
D. Mustard Honey Turkey Breast
Day 27
B. Spiced Apples
L. Diabetic-Friendly Meatballs
D. Crab Stuffed Salmon
Day 28
B. Roasted Peanut Butter Squash
L. Fried Green Beans with Pecorino Romano
D. Air Fried Salmon

Day 29
B. Honey Brussels Sprouts
L. Chicken Casserole
D. Breaded Sea Scallops
Day 30
B. Mini Pizza
L. Thyme Turkey Breast
D. Tomato Basil Scallops

Made in the USA
Las Vegas, NV
18 October 2023